WITHDRAWN

BUILDING THE SERVICE-BASED LIBRARY WEB SITE

A Step-by-Step Guide to Design and Options

Kristen L. Garlock and Sherry Piontek

American Library Association
Chicago and London
1996

D1285747

Cover design: Richmond Jones

Printed on 50-pound Victor Offset, a pH-neutral stock, and
bound in 10-point C1S cover stock by Victor Graphics, Inc.

The paper used in this publication meets the minimum
requirements of American National Standard for Information
Sciences—Permanence of Paper for Printed Library
Materials, ANSI Z39.48-1992. ∞

ISBN: 0-8389-0674-5

Printed in the United States of America.

00 99 98 97 96   5 4 3 2 1

Table of Contents

Preface

The World Wide Web, with its captivating multimedia features and hypertext capabilities, has captured the public's imagination, bringing millions of new users to the Internet. People in the business of managing information resources, including those of us in libraries, are paying especially close attention to this new medium. The Web is a valuable tool for the mission of libraries. Web pages can present information in an organized and easy-to-use manner. With more and more libraries as well as major commercial online services offering Internet access to the public, the Web reaches an ever expanding community. We believe that all library staff should be thinking about how the Web might be used to improve library services. Therefore, our goal is to present a non-technical, accessible introduction to what the Web can do. We have drawn on our experiences as librarians and Web site designers and have also featured the best library applications of the Web—from the sophisticated to the simply clever.

As members of the group that developed the University of Michigan University Library Home Page, we gained useful experience in WWW development and organization. The University of Michigan, with over 51,000 students, has a large, decentralized library system with over 7 million volumes and over 400 professional and support staff. Creating a representative home page for a system this large presented a unique challenge. Group members spent much time intensively experimenting with HTML, design issues, information gathering, and overall promotion.

The project was initiated by the University's Digital Library Program, a joint effort of its Information Technology Division, the School of Information and Library Studies, and the University Library. The program seeks to create a campus information network which is comprehensive, coherent, and coordinated. The home page is one of several projects developed to carry out this mission.

The University of Michigan University Library Home Page was created by a six-member team working under the program director, Wendy Lougee. The team worked from August to December of 1994, gathering information, designing the home page structure, and composing the WWW pages.

The resulting home page can be found at **http://www.lib.umich.edu/**.

The purpose was, and is, to establish a "library gateway" on the World Wide Web which would:

- Provide information about the library system

- Provide a platform for the library to become an information provider and producer through the creation of electronic exhibits and through the development and organization of local digital resources

- Establish links to other resources on the Internet

The team assembled to create the home page included librarians and library science students. Their combined talents included experience with HTML tagging, skill in developing graphics, and a basic familiarity with the Internet and the evaluation of its resources.

During the initial stages of development, the team concentrated on the first objective, providing information about the library. Members carried this out by gathering comprehensive descriptive information and organizing it into a framework. The team focused on describing the various facilities of the library and its operations, using information gathered through individual interviews and the collection of existing print materials.

Elements that emerged in this process, and which were eventually incorporated, included:

- An overall library description

- Campus and library maps

- Selected policy statements

- Hours of operation

- A personnel directory, including photos of staff

- Unit descriptions including information about collections, special resources and services, photographs, floor plans, and contact people

- Representative graphics and video clips

- Digital resources

The remaining objectives of providing a platform for digital resources and establishing links to other Internet resources are ongoing, and this process will continue as digital resources emerge.

In the course of writing this book, we have benefited from the work and support of several people. Kim Bayer, Chris Poterala, Phil Ray, and Deborah Torres, our fellow University of Michigan Library home page team members, not only worked to create a useful web site, but were great sources of information. We would also like to thank Wendy Lougee and Pat Hodges of the University of Michigan Digital Library program for their support and advice during this project. Our many friends and colleagues at the University of Michigan who offered suggestions and assistance are also much appreciated.

We also owe a debt to the community of libraries on the Web. Their contributions are evident in the many home page examples and recommended Web sites included in this book. If you are a veteran of the Web, you understand that some of these sites may disappear or change their URLs. But for every site you miss, you'll find many more on your own by actively browsing and asking your colleagues "What's cool?" Consider the ideas in this book a starting point, inspiration for your own creativity.

1 The Home Page Advantage

In a short time virtually everyone will know at least something about the Internet. Books, magazine articles, and news programs feature constant discussions of the Information Superhighway. For example, in 1995 *Time Magazine* devoted an entire issue to an examination of cyberspace. Major news shows on National Public Radio (NPR) provide e-mail addresses for listener response, such as **atc@npr.org** for "All Things Considered." NPR also has a multimedia Internet site for visitors to access. Bookstores now offer more books about the Internet than one could possibly ever read, and professional library journals are now filled with articles about the Internet.

There is good reason for the intensive coverage. Widespread use and knowledge of the Internet are growing at an astounding rate. In its August 1995 survey (**http:// info.isoc.org:80/infosvc/press/ 020895press.txt**), the Internet Society ("the International Organization for global cooperation and coordination for the Internet, its internetworking technologies, and applications," **http://www.isoc.org/**) counted 6.6 million host computers in 106 countries and reported a 37 percent growth rate in Internet use for the first half of 1995. And, unsurprising to any Internet user, the majority of these hosts were World Wide Web host computers. The World Wide Web, developed at CERN laboratories in Geneva, has become the preferred interface to the Internet. Originally created for use by scientific communities, in 1991 it became available for use by anyone with an Internet connection. The Web, unlike previous tools such as gopher, presents not only text, but sound, graphics, and videos through one interface. This combination of flexibility and power has attracted an enormous audience.

Internet users encompass a wide spectrum. Businesses, publishers, universities, and other producers of information now offer their services and products on sites at various Internet locations. Here are some Internet addresses that may sound familiar:

- TimeWarner Publishers (**http:// www.pathfinder.com/**) — includes excerpts from *Time* and *People* magazines.

- National Public Radio (**http://www.npr.org/**) — includes information on member stations and how to order transcripts

- The Library of Congress (**http://lcweb.loc.gov/**) — includes links to special exhibits, historical collections, and "Thomas" (legislative information on the Internet)

- American Library Association (**http://www.ala.org/**) — includes information about ALA services, divisions and programs

And there are many more government, university, and business sites on the Internet, not to mention millions of individuals, "surfing" this enticing information environment.

So, What Is the World Wide Web?

The World Wide Web (WWW) is a digital, networked information system. It consists of electronic files and documents tagged with codes from a standard set of guidelines known as "HyperText Markup Language," more commonly referred to as HTML. These marked-up documents incorporate hypertext links that allow users to move easily to other points in a document, or to entirely different documents, by selecting a highlighted phrase or object.

Personal WWW documents are commonly referred to as "home pages" or, sometimes, "web pages." They are created by individuals or organizations such as those mentioned above, to present their own information or to serve as collections of other Internet resources. A collection of home pages, all usually interconnected and located on the same server is often called a "web site." Other phrases you might hear to

describe the WWW are "webspace," "cyberspace," or just the "web." Terminology for this technology is still evolving, but all of these phrases refer to the creation of HTML documents and their display on the World Wide Web.

To directly access information on the World Wide Web, the user enters an address (known as a Uniform Resource Locator, or URL) into a type of software called a browser, such as lynx, Mosaic or Netscape. These addresses link the user to host computers and their individual files, which are then displayed on the user's personal workstation. With the appropriate software, users can read documents, view pictures, listen to sound, and retrieve information from anywhere in the world.

The skills involved in creating these documents can be learned easily, which has fueled enormous popularity and growth of the WWW. In fact, a few hours spent with *A Beginner's Guide to HTML* (**http://www.ncsa.uiuc.edu/General/Internet/WWW/HTMLPrimer.html**) will enable you to create a basic home page.

What Does This Have to Do with Your Library?

Although new web pages are created every day, truly useful and well-organized pages are rare. Librarians trained in evaluating and organizing information can make their mark by creating useful sites with information of quality. As a librarian, you are well positioned to take advantage of the World Wide Web phenomenon. You may be familiar with the Internet, perhaps having already used e-mail, listservs, and gophers. The World Wide Web is just another tool that you can use to access familiar resources, discover new information, and display information of your own.

Many libraries already have established web sites. Examining these provides an idea of what a library web site can look like and what it can do. To find these sites, you can start with Thomas Dowling's list of university library home pages from around the world (**http://www.lib.washington.edu/ ~tdowling/libweb.html**), which is organized geographically. He also includes a list of library-related companies, such as Dialog, Mead Data Central, and University Microfilms, Inc.

To look at a web site offering several different types of library services, see the Internet Public Library (**http://www.ipl.org**), a WWW library modeled after a traditional public library. Within its reference department it includes a link to the St. Joseph County Public Library (South Bend, Indiana) list of public libraries that have created sites for the WWW. (This list can also be directly accessed at **http://sjcpl.lib.in.us/homepage/ PublicLibraries/PublicLibraryServers.html**).

School libraries are also establishing web presences. For example, the Virginia L.

Murray Elementary School Library (**http:// pen1.pen.k12.va.us/Anthology/Div/ Albemarle/Schools/MurrayElem/Library/ sandy.home.html**) in Ivy, Virginia has a page which is part of the school's site, and contains book reviews written by students, as well as resources for educators (Figure 1.1).

You, Too, Can Create a Home Page

After you have had the opportunity to examine other library home pages, it is time to think about developing one for your own library. There are many reasons for creating a home page, and many approaches which you can take. As you have seen, libraries of all types have already established WWW sites, and more are appearing all the time.

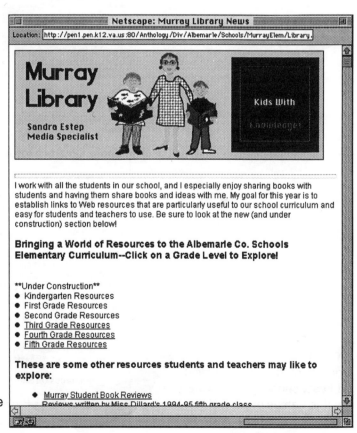

FIGURE 1.1
Student-contributed book reviews are a part of this elementary school site.

Presenting Local Information

Basic Library Information

A common reason for creating a library home page is to make basic library information available on the Internet (Figure 1.2). Frequent requests for information such as hours of operation, contact people, address, phone number, and library policies can be answered on a web page. If you already have a pamphlet, brochure or handout with this information, you can easily convert it to an HTML document using a word-processing application or an HTML editor. You can also design an entirely different document containing both text and multimedia components.

You can do a lot to make basic information more interesting to those viewing it on your web page. Instead of a simple list of names, phone numbers, and e-mail addresses in a staff directory, you can add staff pictures and direct e-mail links so a user can send a message immediately. You could include a sound file with brief remarks. (For an example of a sound file greeting, see the Swarthmore College home page at **http://www.swarthmore.edu/**, where you can hear the president welcoming visitors.) An image of your library on your opening page establishes a sense of familiarity for those visiting your site. In some cases, short video clips of staff may be used. For an example of this, see Figure 1.3.

FIGURE 1.2
Contact information, including address, phone number, library hours, and the names of contact people, is included in this basic page.

FIGURE 1.3
A staff movie helps introduce the Film and Video Library Home Page at the University of Michigan.

In implementing a home page, avoid cluttering it with too much detail about your library. Too much basic information works against the design of a home page and confuses users. Basic information works best if it is simple, prominently placed on the page (preferably at the top), and always kept up to date.

Creating New Ways to Access Library Information and Services

In addition to providing basic information, WWW technology can be used to present existing library resources in new ways. Unlike the limits imposed by print reference

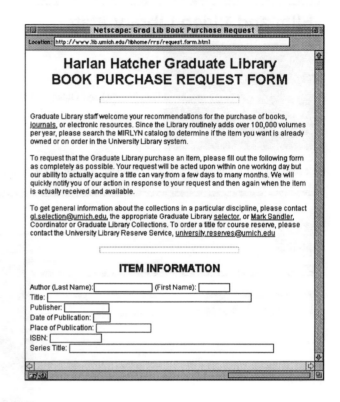

FIGURE 1.4
Different access points to the same information

materials or free-standing computer workstations within the library, the World Wide Web provides patrons with multiple entry points for accessing resources from their home computers.

Entry points to the information in your site can be placed wherever you feel they make the most sense, and you can create as many entry points for a piece of information as you think are necessary. For example, a book request form (Figure 1.4) allowing patrons to suggest books for purchase could, logically, be reached from a page describing the library's collections. But it also might make sense to link the book request form to a "Question and Answer" page, or to a description of a subject selector. You can link the form to any or all of these locations.

Patron access can be improved by directly linking an online catalog to a library home page (Figure 1.5). This makes it much easier for your regular patrons to find materials. Patrons avoid having to come in and wait for a computer terminal, and an online catalog enables them to check on the availability of an item before making the trip to your building. Such a home page also makes the catalog available to remote users or to those physically unable to access the library who would like to explore your holdings.

Another option is to create an actual WWW interface for your online catalog (Figure 1.6). Recent versions of most WWW browsers have a fill-out forms capability, which allows libraries to create and specify fields for input or searching by users. In-

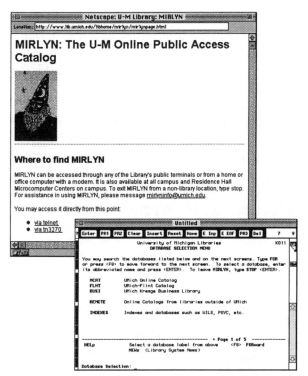

FIGURE 1.5
Connection to MIRLYN, the University of
Michigan online library catalog

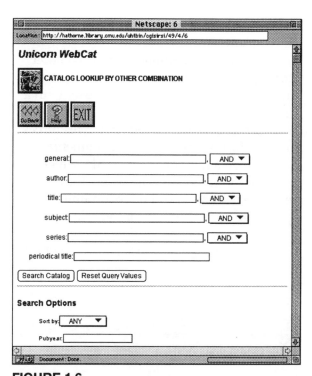

FIGURE 1.6
Carnegie-Mellon University's online catalog,
which uses fill-out forms as interfaces

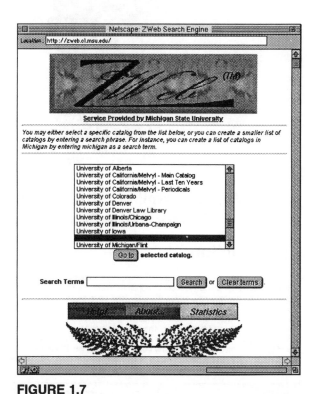

FIGURE 1.7
ZWeb is Michigan State University's gateway to
its own online catalog, as well as library catalogs
at other institutions.

creasingly, libraries are using fill-out forms as
interfaces for online catalogs. Figure 1.6 is
one example.

Michigan State University has taken the
use of fill-out forms even further. "ZWeb" is
the school's WWW gateway to library catalogs (Figure 1.7). According to the background information about ZWeb (**http://
petroglyph.cl.msu.edu/~tigger/Projects/**),
"Extensions are being pursued in support of
CD-ROM databases as well as other network
information. One of the primary motivations
behind this software is to allow for the
expansion of library catalogs into multimedia
and online document retrieval."

Behind the scenes, a script (commonly a
UNIX-based program) provides the framework for the search functions while linking

the user's WWW software to the online catalog software.

By making an online catalog available through a home page, online documentation and help files appear simultaneously with a link to the actual resource. Print resources, as well as more traditional electronic resources, lack the format and depth of documentation available in a hypertext online file, which can be linked to the same page where the actual resource is located, and offers unlimited space and opportunities for hyperlinks to other areas of documentation.

A home page may also showcase library resources. The ability of the WWW to include images, sounds, movie clips, and text in one presentation offers new opportunities for displaying exhibits, special collections (Figure 1.8), or library tours. Videos of a storytime, photographs of the library, and oral narration can all be successfully integrated into a single web presentation. Such a presentation not only provides more excitement than a comparable print version, but expands the audience by making your resources available to patrons regardless of their physical location or your hours of operation.

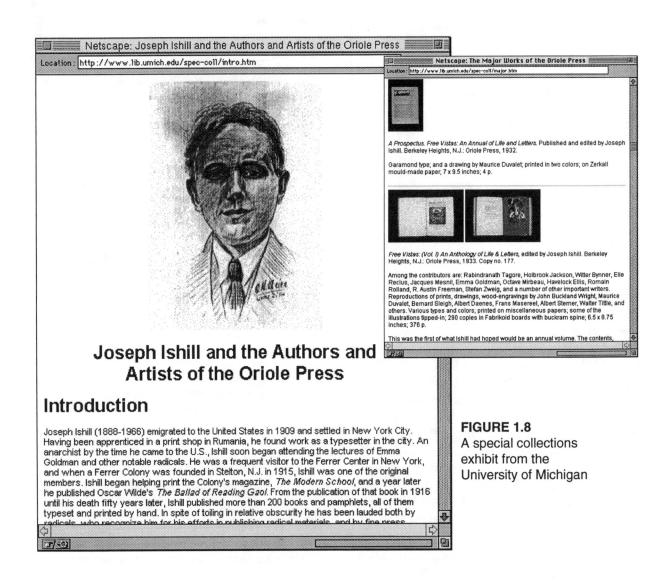

FIGURE 1.8
A special collections exhibit from the University of Michigan

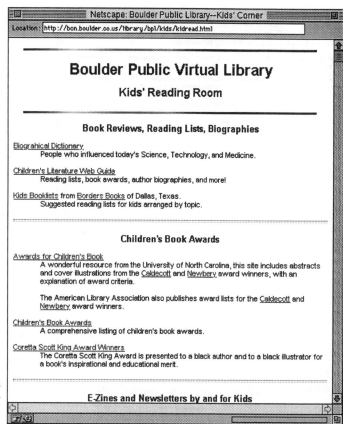

Location: http://bcn.boulder.co.us/library/bpl/kids/kidread.html

Boulder Public Virtual Library
Kids' Reading Room

Book Reviews, Reading Lists, Biographies

Biograhical Dictionary
  People who influenced today's Science, Technology, and Medicine.

Children's Literature Web Guide
  Reading lists, book awards, author biographies, and more!

Kids Booklists from Borders Books of Dallas, Texas.
  Suggested reading lists for kids arranged by topic.

Children's Book Awards

Awards for Children's Book
  A wonderful resource from the University of North Carolina, this site includes abstracts
  and cover illustrations from the Caldecott and Newbery award winners, with an
  explanation of award criteria.

  The American Library Association also publishes award lists for the Caldecott and
  Newbery award winners.

Children's Book Awards
  A comprehensive listing of children's book awards.

Coretta Scott King Award Winners
  The Coretta Scott King Award is presented to a black author and to a black illustrator for
  a book's inspirational and educational merit.

E-Zines and Newsletters by and for Kids

FIGURE 1.9
The "Kids' Reading Room" is an example of how Internet resources may be arranged in a digital library format for a targeted audience.

Creating New Information Resources and Services

Producing a WWW home page can also spur development of new resources and services that depend on the WWW for their form and structure. One such new concept is the "digital library"—a library not limited by physical constraints such as space, geographic location, or specific type of computer system. Many digital libraries combine different formats of electronic information, including text, images, and video, and seek to make the contents of the library available to a wide range of users, from elementary school children to university faculty members.

Digital libraries often incorporate resource-sharing between the library and other organizations. The National Science Foundation, for example, currently funds six digital library projects ranging from a digital video library system to be created by Carnegie-Mellon University to a digital library with a focus on environmental information at the University of California, Berkeley. A description of these NSF-sponsored projects and a bibliography of materials regarding digital libraries can be found at **http://www.nlc-bnc.ca/ifla/services/ diglib.htm**.

Digital libraries do not have to be multimillion-dollar projects at large universities. A digital library can be as simple as a home page linked to a collection of electronic texts, databases, and other existing Internet resources. For example, the Boulder Public Library (Boulder Colorado) has created a "virtual library," a section of which is geared toward children—the "Kids' Reading Room" (Figure 1.9).

What distinguishes a digital library from a hotlist or bookmark file is the consid-

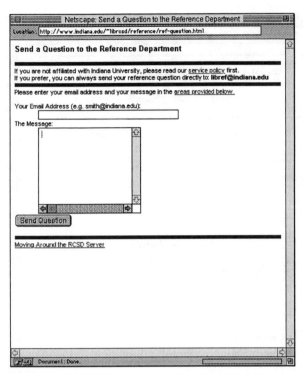

FIGURE 1.10
A fill-out form allows patrons to request reference services from the Indiana University Library.

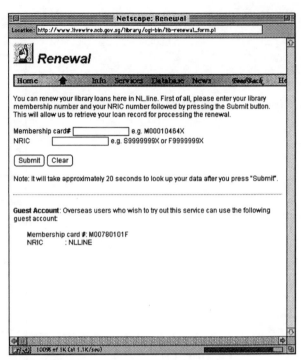

FIGURE 1.11
Another fill-out form provides for remote renewal of library materials.

eration given to issues such as who the audience or "patrons" of this digital library will be, which materials are to be included, and how the library will be structured and maintained. For example, the Clark Public Library (Clark, New Jersey), in building up a collection of subject guides (**http://www.intac.com/~kgs/subject.html**), evaluates and organizes materials with librarians in mind. The time and effort put into evaluative enterprises such as this by professional librarians ensures that resources are organized cohesively into true libraries rather than being simple lists of Internet resources.

Using a Home Page as an Interactive Tool

As mentioned earlier, fill-out forms are one example of the Web's interactive potential. We have already mentioned fill-out forms as an interface to an online catalog. Fill-out forms can also be used as tools for feedback

and services. Requests for purchases, reservation of library material, and general library suggestions are all possible uses. Some more advanced libraries use forms for interlibrary loan services, circulation activities, and reference questions (Figure 1.10).

The University of Singapore Library uses interactive forms which allow patrons to make queries about their borrower status and due dates, renew borrowed items, ask reference questions, or recommend items for purchase (**http://www.livewire.ncb.gov.sg/library/cgi-bin/libservice.pl**) (Figure 1.11).

Linking to Remote Information

Library home pages also serve as a gateway to remote information. The WWW not only lends itself well as a showcase for local information; it also allows the library to connect with information and resources from around the world, thereby making them available to patrons.

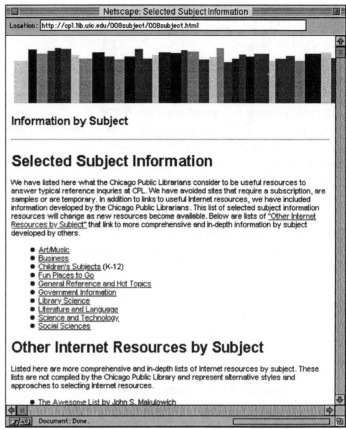

FIGURE 1.12
The Chicago Public Library's online reference service guides patrons to Internet resources arranged by subject.

Frequently Used Information

Library staff members currently keep hotlists and bookmark files of frequently used resources for their personal use, not usually making them available to others. However, a home page of frequently used sites organized using a subject scheme can facilitate better access to Internet resources than a bookmark file or hotlist (Figure 1.12). Many libraries with web sites have been creating sections or individual pages specifically for online reference collections. Unfortunately, the hotlist and bookmark features of current WWW browsers remain rudimentary tools that are sometimes difficult to use for organizing large numbers of heavily requested resources.

A page of WWW resources kept on hand for answering frequently asked questions serves as the electronic equivalent of "ready reference" tools. The same evaluative

criteria involved in selecting ready references should be used in selecting these resources. Although reference staff may primarily select and maintain these resources, other specialists may also play a role in their selection.

Clearly, using a home page to link to outside resources expands the library collection by including information resources and tools which would have otherwise been unavailable.

A Place for Exploration

We have discussed several directions taken by libraries creating web sites, including the presentation of basic information, the creation of new access mechanisms and resources, the implementation of an interactive home page, and the collection and organization of remote Internet resources. Utilizing one or a combination of these approaches helps provide information to your patrons more quickly and accurately, and enables libraries to respond more quickly to patrons' suggestions. It also establishes your library's presence on the Internet.

Taking time now to establish a web site for your library is a good idea for these reasons alone. But, as mentioned earlier, the WWW is growing at an incredible rate. The new technology that accompanies this growth will be understood best by those who become familiar with the technology as it is now. Producing a web site will teach you how the Internet works, and this behind-the-scenes knowledge will help you anticipate future changes in information technology. In other words, the longer you wait to begin a web site, the further behind you will fall, and the more you will have to learn when you finally decide to begin.

Furthermore, the process of creating a web site plays an important role in laying groundwork for the development of techno-logical skills in your organization. We found that those who worked on the University of Michigan University Library home page refined their computer skills and became well-versed in WWW technology, learning about client-server applications, Internet navigation tools such as FTP and telnet, and the arrival of new WWW browsers and related software. Those involved in the project also came away with a broader perspective of the Internet as a whole, skills in finding and evaluating Internet resources, and great enthusiasm for using it in their work. This enthusiasm has spread through-out the library system as librarians in various departments have taken it upon themselves to begin work on their individual portions of the home page. Not only does a web site provide a valuable resource, but its creation may act as a catalyst for staff development by providing a platform and an impetus for the development of future skills.

Creating a web site to present both local and remote information not only provides patrons and staff with a wider variety of resources and with multiple access points to these resources, but also leads inevitably to more publicity, visibility and credibility for your library. It encourages staff to learn more about technology, and keeps your organiza-tion abreast of future changes. A library web site can be more than just a nice home page. It can be a gateway to new worlds of infor-mation.

2 Start with a Plan

As you have seen, a library home page can serve as a simple informational outlet or as a complex, service-based resource. Whether simple or complex, the first steps you take will be the same. You need to start by choosing an approach and coming up with a tentative timeline, and then start thinking about some policies for your web site.

Step 1: Choosing an Approach

In Chapter 1, we listed several different approaches which can be taken when designing a library web site: putting up basic information, adding local resources, creating new resources for the WWW platform, linking to remote resources, or a combination of any of these. The first step in creating a home page is to determine which of these options you will incorporate into your page. Your choice will depend on several factors, including:

- the amount of administrative support you have

- the availability of equipment and technical support

- availability of staff to work on the site

- your intended audience

Administrative Support

A basic requirement for creating a web site or home page is administrative support and encouragement. Such a project requires time and resources, and you will need backing. Your administrator's vision will influence the approach you take by the time and/or funds he or she is willing to allocate for it. So, in a very real way, this support is basic. You will also need reassurance that time can be allotted for the maintenance (and, if you decide it is appropriate, the expansion) of the project.

Another reason for securing administrative support is that your library's approach will impact its image on the Internet. Examining your library's mission statement, and perhaps drafting a set of goals for your web site, will shape your library's thinking about its cyberspace identity. Your library will have a public presence on the web, and you, with input from your administration, should consider how your mission statement addresses this new area of service.

Many libraries regard web site activities as extensions of their traditional services and, therefore, as fitting naturally into their original mission statements. Some of these libraries publish their traditional mission statements on the web without any modifications. One of these is the Westerville Public Library, in Westerville, Ohio, which makes the following available on its web page:

> The Westerville Public Library provides materials, programs and service to residents of all ages in Franklin and Delaware counties to assist in their pursuit of information and resources to meet their educational, professional and personal needs. Particular emphasis is placed on delivering quality reference services and providing popular materials of high interest to the residents of the Westerville School District. The library also serves to stimulate young children's interest and appreciation for reading and learning.
>
> **(http://www.wpl.lib.oh.us/ mission_statement.html)**

Other libraries recognize that the principles of their mission will remain the same, but they draft specific policies addressing the uniqueness of delivering services via the World Wide Web and the Internet. For example, the Public Library of Charlotte and Mecklenburg County in Charlotte, North Carolina, has posted its Internet Access Policy, in which it relates its web services to its mission statement:

> For PLCMC's purposes, the Internet is seen as another tool or resource to be used in accordance with the central goal of the 'ibrary's Mission:

> ... to be a principal provider of books, information, and informational materials to all the communities of Charlotte/ Mecklenburg ...

> While recognizing that the Internet provides access to a vast array of tools and resources for different age levels and points-of-view, PLCMC does not act in place or in absence of the parent and is not responsible for enforcing any restrictions which a parent or guardian may place on a minor's use of this resource.

> The accuracy of information gained through this source is the responsibility of each originator/producer. Therefore, PLCMC does not guarantee the accuracy of non-PLCMC information obtained through the Internet.

> Users are required to adhere to any posted use or time limitations.

> **(http://www.plcmc.lib.nc.us/main/ policy.html)**

Still other libraries have drafted mission statements specifically for their web services, such as the one composed by the Milton Public Library, in Milton, Massachusetts:

> The mission of the Milton Public Library is to bring a new library and full access to the World Wide Web to all the people of Milton so as to effectively meet their cultural, educational, vocational and recreational needs.

> **(http://www.tiac.net/users/mpl/)**

Or this one from the Abbot Public Library in Marblehead, Massachusetts:

> The mission of the Abbot Public Library is to serve all residents of the town of Marblehead as a center for education, culture, recreation, and information through its collections, programs, resources, and personnel. The library serves individuals of

all ages and abilities, businesses, organizations, and governmental units. Our purpose is to provide an opportunity for all to inform and educate themselves. The staff attempts to identify community needs and meet them whenever possible. The introduction of new technologies, material formats, and programs is consistent with this goal.

(**http://www.marblehead.com/commun/ library/**)

The public display of a statement about your intentions for your web site—whether it is your existing mission statement, an additional policy or goal statement, or an entirely new mission written specifically for the web—will not only announce to others what your intentions are, but, when written with your administration, clarifies for everyone what the role of your web site will be. This can help you envision what your approach should be—whether your site should present basic information or a much broader range of services.

Equipment

Getting ready for production requires planning for equipment. You will need to consider three main categories of equipment before beginning a web site—network access, hardware, and software. Options for each are available to suit any size of library, and almost any size of budget. The following discussion offers some basic descriptions of the equipment you will need, giving examples of how different libraries have approached the equipment issue. For resources providing more detailed information about equipment, see Appendix A.

Network Access

The first equipment issue you will need to resolve is network access. Network access means that you will be able to create documents and make them available on the Internet, and provide access to other resources on the Internet. There are two kinds of network access: direct network access and dial-up network access.

Direct Network Access

Direct access means a direct line from your library to the Internet. You can own your own network access line, or you can subscribe to one through a commercial service provider. Direct network access has many advantages over dial-up access, such as being faster and more reliable. Such a connection is faster because it does not compete for the limited number of telephone lines available and because it is a much more powerful connection. Direct network connections are generally more reliable because, instead of telephone lines, the system uses a "dedicated" network line. There are many different kinds of direct network access. Ethernet and ISDN (Integrated Services Digital Network) lines are some examples with which you may be familiar.

Dial-Up Access

Dial-up Internet access may be obtained through both commercial and nonprofit organizations. Commercial organizations offering network services are often called "Internet providers." A dial-up access package generally includes dial-up access to a network, e-mail, and storage space for documents. Also included may be some technical support and equipment (hardware and software).

Smaller-sized public libraries or libraries in small schools, may be able to gain network access through a nearby university, college, or community organization. Check with the technology division of a local college or organization for more information on such possibilities.

Hardware

In addition to network access, you will need to plan for your hardware needs. All platforms—DOS, Windows, Macintosh, and UNIX—can be used as servers and for creating WWW documents. These machines also do not need to be the most recent models to create a successful web site (Figure 2.1).

Though computers are more powerful and faster, a server can still be run on a fairly old and not very powerful machine. For optimum performance, you may decide to upgrade such equipment.

Software

Along with network access and hardware, you will need different kinds of software to create your web site. Much of the work can be accomplished with minimal software, most of which you probably already have. Software essentials for a web project are server software (necessary only if you are using your own server, but not with dial-up network access), a word-processing applica-

FIGURE 2.1
Even an older, less powerful computer, like a Mac IIcx, can be used as a server.

tion, and a graphics application. Server software is available for every platform, and allows you to run a WWW server from a variety of machines. Word-processing applications are used for the HTML work, and graphics applications are used to manipulate and create images and icons.

Server Software

Server software allows client software (a WWW browser or other Internet application) to interact with the information on your server. As mentioned earlier, UNIX, DOS, Windows, and Macintosh machines can all be used as servers for your web site. Both commercial and freeware/shareware server software is available, and many packages for Macs and DOS/Windows machines are quite easy to install. To maintain a server no longer requires a UNIX whiz. For a great list of both free and commercial server software, see the World Wide Web Consortium server software page (**http://www.w3.org/pub/www/ Servers.html**).

HTML Work

All HTML work can be done successfully using basic word-processing software, such as Microsoft Word, WordPerfect, Simpletext, and UNIX text editors such as vi and pico. Specialized software, known as HTML converters and HTML editors, can also be used to create HTML documents. HTML converters operate by taking a document formatted by a word-processing program and translating the formatted text into a tagged HTML document. HTML editors resemble word processing programs, but instead of tagging a document by hand, you can use menus to insert tags directly into your document.

Currently, HTML converters possess limited ability to recognize more than basic formatting, while some HTML editors are quite complex and include a wide range of HTML tags. There are many different kinds of HTML converters and editors, many are available through the Internet as shareware and freeware applications. One example is HTML Web Weaver (Figure 2.2).

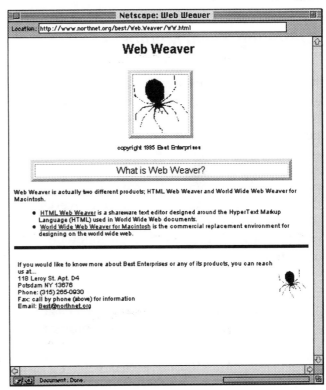

FIGURE 2.2
Web Weaver is an HTML editor available for use as shareware on the Internet.

Graphics Work

Graphics work is best done using a drawing or paint application, or other software used to manipulate images. You will probably want to use graphics software to create headers, buttons, and icons for your pages. Creating images for your documents does not require you to be an artist, but you do need to have the correct software. Such shareware graphics programs as GIFConverter may serve some of your graphics needs; however, you will most likely need to invest in some graphics programs such as Adobe Photoshop or MacPaint.

Remember, you will not only have to determine the equipment needs for web site production, you will have to be able to tell your patrons what kind of equipment they will need to access the web site. A helpful example of this approach to equipment planning is the *Action Plan for Michigan Libraries: Recommendations from the Michigan Library Association Task Force on the National Information Infrastructure* (**http://www.sils.umich.edu/~durrance/MLA/mla.html**).

Choosing Team Members

After determining the availability of support and equipment, and after identifying your audience, you need to decide who is going to be responsible for the creation of the web site. The number of people and their availability to work on it will impact your approach to the site. You will have to balance the availability of staff time with your overall plans for the home page, so you will need to make some decisions based on the following considerations:

- Do you have limited staff? If so, then you might want to start with just a basic home page that includes, at a minimum,

contact information and a description of some basic library services and collections.

- Do you have a team of people with interest and the time needed to create a more extensive home page? Then you may want present local information and develop a collection of Internet resources for your users.

- Do you have the luxury of a staff able to dedicate a large portion of working time to the development of a complex home page? You may, then, want to plan a more ambitious project which could include, in addition to the features mentioned above, fill-out forms for service requests, the creation of new network resources, and much more.

Once you have determined how much staff time can be devoted, you can start looking for the particular staff members you would like to include on the project.

What qualifications should these team members have? To determine this, consider what needs to be done throughout the course of the project. A large amount of time will be devoted to HTML tagging, of course, and it would be helpful if those working on the site had some experience with HTML. If this is not possible, many training manuals exist for those who want to learn, and mastering the basic principles takes little time. [See Appendix A.] A good method for learning HTML involves finding sites which you like and then viewing the tagging on the files within those sites by using the "view source" option on your browser. With one of the basic HTML references as a guide, experiment with these tags until you become familiar with what they do.

In addition to basic HTML tagging, there will be other important activities. Depending on the extent of your web site plans, these can include:

- collecting existing brochures and hand-outs and deciding if they can be adapted to a web presentation

- interviewing staff for information about their departments and functions

- creating, editing, and moving text files on a server

- creating or modifying graphics with imaging software

- creating logical organizational schemes for the presentation of data

- experimenting with design choices

In assigning these tasks, it is important to choose staff comfortable and familiar with the WWW who have spent some time browsing and evaluating resources on the Internet. Such experience develops the best understanding of how hypertext documents on the WWW work, what materials are most suitable for a hypertext presentation, and how to organize materials for ease of patron access.

Creating basic WWW pages requires some basic computer experience, primarily in text editing and/or word processing. Some UNIX experience, at least enough to move files onto the server where they will be accessed, can be helpful. However, a system administrator can take care of these functions. For more elaborate projects, you may want to consult a professional about advanced techniques, such as scripting.

Home page projects benefit from the counsel of someone who has experience working with graphics, primarily with digital images and with imaging software. There are ways around this, however; many sites on the Web freely offer images for users to take. See Appendix A for a list of such sites.

The only truly necessary criteria for all team members are their enjoyment navigating the Internet and willingness to experiment a little. Much can be accomplished with even the minimal skills mentioned here, and working on the WWW site will be a learning process for anyone involved.

The Team Approach

Although a lot of web sites are successfully created by one individual, for practical reasons we recommend using a team. At the beginning, there is a lot of work involved in gathering information, organizing it, and preparing it for presentation. An individual working independently may overlook areas of information that could be included in the site. Also, one person may easily overlook mistakes, whereas members of a group are more likely to proofread for each other. Furthermore, if the person is in control of the site, and then has to leave the organization, it creates a greater problem than if one member of a team departs.

Using a group also creates a positive perception of the project. If several staff members are involved, others will be more likely to see it as a community project, and may be more willing to contribute information and suggestions. Making this a team project can be the best way to encourage large-scale participation, to ensure the inclusion of different viewpoints, and to draw upon a large range of potential talents.

Give some thought to choosing the members of the team. Keep in mind the types of tasks outlined above, realizing that these may be suited to certain individuals. Ask staff members about particular areas in which they may be interested, and plan accordingly. Tell them what you hope they will bring to the group and see if their perceptions match yours.

How much time will it take the group at first? Group meetings will probably happen more often at the beginning of the project, and then less frequently as members start getting involved with their individual sections. Because this is a networked, interactive project, a lot of work can be done online. Once the basic decisions are worked out, individuals can put their work up on the web for others in the group to see and revise.

Within the group, it helps to have a designated team leader or liaison who will keep track of what everyone is doing and how it all fits together. This should help the team avoid duplication of work. This person may also serve as a contact person for other staff members who provides progress reports for those interested.

Organization of teamwork varies with the people involved. Individual team members might want to take responsibility for a single area of the site to research and develop in detail, or they might want to perform a specific task consistently throughout the project. For example, one team member may want to work with the reference area of the library. This person could interview the staff within the reference area, collect relevant reference area handouts, organize this information with help from reference staff, design the page, and present it as a completed section. Another group member might want to design the graphics for the entire site, regardless of department. This person could ensure that graphics throughout the site are consistent and informative. Either approach works, as long as all members of the group understand where the responsibilities lie. A clear definition of duties makes it much easier to keep everyone enthusiastic.

Audience

Once you have obtained administrative backing, equipment, and some staff to work on your site, you must consider your audience. With Internet services, just as with any other new library service, you must keep in mind the needs of both patrons and staff.

Take the time to specifically identify your target audience. Theoretically, your work becomes available to everyone who uses the Web, but chances are that you will be aiming toward a smaller, more identifiable group of regular users. Think of patrons who tend to request electronic documents, who are computer-savvy, and who you can imagine would use your page. Would they look for basic information about the library, or resources beyond the library? Remember to include library staff among your audience. What resources on the Internet do they use now? If you had a web site, how would they use it? Are they aware of government documents on the Web, or of subject-based resources? What type of connectivity do you and your staff use to access the Internet? If you and your patrons have only vt100 access, you don't really need a lot of images on your pages. If you have high-powered equipment, but you feel that your patrons do not, you might not want to create too much that they cannot view.

Summary

Your initial plans for your web site will be determined by the support you receive for this project, the computer and software you have to work on, the staff selected to work on the site, and by the characteristics known about your audience. You should have a general idea after communicating with team members about their thoughts on it, how extensive your web site or home page will be. Start listing the ideas. Once they are in place, you can start thinking of a timeline, and can start setting some preliminary goals for the team.

Step 2: Setting up a Project Timeline

As you think about your timeline and some preliminary deadlines, consider the fact that Internet technology changes so quickly, and it is possible to put up and revise information so rapidly, that the traditional long-term planning process with a distant implementation date is not an especially feasible option for a web project. In our experience, a more accelerated process is best. A prototype of the project should be completed early in the process. This prototype can then be presented to selected viewers for comments and revised as needed. This sequence can be repeated infinitely. A home page can be continually revised and improved with feedback from users playing an important role. There is really no need for a long planning phase (Figures 2.3a–2.3c).

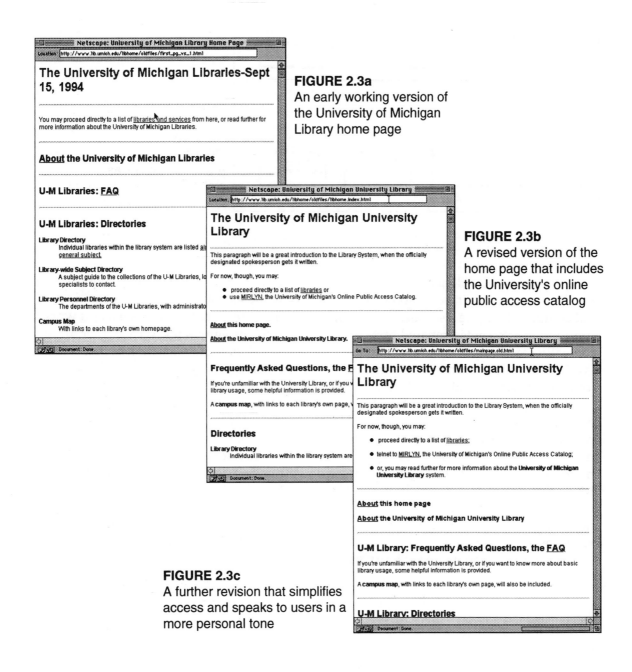

FIGURE 2.3a
An early working version of the University of Michigan Library home page

FIGURE 2.3b
A revised version of the home page that includes the University's online public access catalog

FIGURE 2.3c
A further revision that simplifies access and speaks to users in a more personal tone

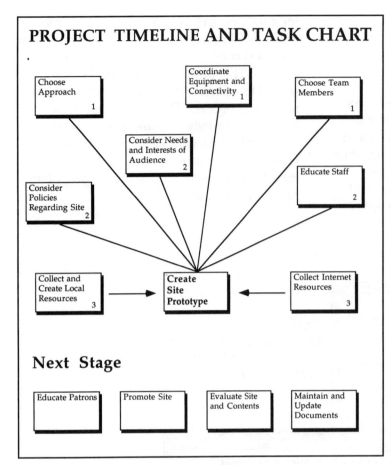

PROJECT TIMELINE AND TASK CHART

Choose Approach 1

Coordinate Equipment and Connectivity 1

Choose Team Members 1

Consider Needs and Interests of Audience 2

Educate Staff 2

Consider Policies Regarding Site 2

Collect and Create Local Resources 3

Create Site Prototype

Collect Internet Resources 3

Next Stage

Educate Patrons

Promote Site

Evaluate Site and Contents

Maintain and Update Documents

FIGURE 2.4
A web site begins as a prototype that is continually revised and improved

That said, you still need to set up some deadlines for getting information together and composed (Figure 2.4). Basic operating information often gets prepared first since it is usually readily available. Most libraries have a hand-out or even a sign with open hours and basic circulation policies.

Descriptive material about the library is usually the next piece to fall into place. This may require more composition, and some research, depending on how much you want to provide, and on how large your organiza-tion is. Some libraries have included their histories, a description of the area in which they're located, and descriptions of their buildings and collections.

Adding more about your library's local resources comes next. This requires more work, as you may need to provide descriptions, reformat as necessary, and work on some design issues (see Chapter 5).

Finally, the addition of resources from outside your own library will take place. This requires considering some selection, evaluation, and maintenance issues. These activities need not take place exactly in this order, and none of them will ever be completely finished. After getting a basic page up, and maybe adding local resources, you may want to go back and add descriptive information. You may want to put up links to other resources before your local resources are ready if you feel your audience would find them more useful.

Step 3: Policies Regarding Your Web Site

As with the implementation of any new resources or services, you will want to consider developing policies for your web site. We have already seen examples of policies as they relate to library missions, but you may want to go further and address use and collection activities. It is not too early to start thinking about these issues now. You may want to use already established library policies to address issues regarding your web site, though they may need adaptation to include some of the unique aspects of Internet resources and technology. You may choose to develop entirely new policies specifically for the web site.

Some collection development policies may be adapted to include provisions for the collection development of Internet resources. During the creation of a library home page, many people fall into the trap of making links to resources just because they exist. The ease of creating Internet resources and the lack of editorial control on the Internet leads, unfortunately, to a proliferation of low-quality resources. These facts make a collection development policy for Internet resources very important. A plain list of resources provides little, but an annotated and carefully selected collection of resources based on a formal collection development policy adds considerable value to a library WWW site.

What elements of a traditional collection development policy should be included? Consider the scope of your current collection, and decide what will complement your existing collection. However, a traditional collection development policy should not limit your options.

3 Everybody's Web Site: Consensus and Collaboration

After deciding what level of service to provide on your web site and establishing a team of workers and equipment for the project, it is time to gear up for the production. Your main goal during this part of the process is to get library staff and, perhaps, library board members excited about and involved with the project. To do this you will need to gain general staff support and then start publicizing the project throughout your organization.

Presenting the Plan

The first step will be to communicate your plans for a web site to all staff. Some staff members may be familiar with the Internet and aware of the Web's potential, but many may remain unfamiliar with this new technology. Those working on the home page should take this opportunity to provide some context for a web site and to present the initial ideas, goals, and preliminary designs for the library site.

You should prepare for the presentation by first sketching out your plans on paper. This may sound like a primitive method for such a project, but it can be very helpful. You may discover new ways of looking at the project if you take the time to sketch it out, and this will deepen your understanding of it. The deeper your understanding, the better you will be able to answer questions about the direction of your plans.

For this initial meeting, prepare a handout with the overall goals of the project spelled out. It would be useful to show examples of other well-executed library home pages to staff who have little experience with the Web. Use online demonstrations if the equipment and the right venue for this kind of demonstration are available; otherwise, use paper printouts to illustrate the concepts.

Your staff will have many questions, so try to anticipate these, and try to have your responses prepared. These are some common questions you may hear:

- Why do we need a home page? Isn't our gopher [online catalog, CD-ROM station] enough?

- How can I participate?

- How long will this take?

- Will this project create extra work for me?

- Who will keep it up, or maintain it? (This is an especially important staff concern.)

To answer these and other similar questions, share your original thinking and your timeline. Explain that the team will gather input from all staff, and that the site will be a tool for staff as an addition to other Internet tools. Be ready to highlight the potential benefits of a web site, emphasizing differences between the WWW and such tools as gopher and telnet. Highlight the multimedia potential and the enormous audience the Web attracts. Do your best to provide reasonable answers, even if specific details remain unresolved. Be prepared to explain all the steps of the process as thoroughly as you can. You want to make sure that all staff know what you are talking about.

At this time, put forth some tentative thoughts about maintenance of the site, an extremely important issue. Nothing frustrates staff more than putting a lot of time into a project and watching it die later because of inadequate plans for maintenance. Staff working on the web site will definitely want reassurance that the project will receive both short-term and long-term support. Staff not directly involved with the initial construction of the web site will want to know when they can become involved, and how they will fit into the long-term management of the site. In any case, if staff members see a project die they will lose enthusiasm and it may be difficult to inspire future projects.

Take this opportunity to identify a contact person for the project so staff know who to contact with questions and ideas. Introduce the team members and let them speak about their concepts of the site. Alert staff to the fact that you and the team mem-

bers will be seeking information and assistance from all of them as the project moves along.

After you have presented your general ideas for the site, ask staff to think of specific items that they would like to see included. Have them brainstorm about the possibilities for the web site. Since giving examples helps to generate ideas, offer suggestions and point to the samples you have brought. Some of the first content areas to suggest include:

- An overall description of the library, including collections and hours

- Descriptions of general services, such as circulation and instructional services

- Personnel directories

- Calendar of special events

- A children's area

- The library's newsletter

Let staff know that early work will focus on descriptive sections about the library, and that plans for expansion will come later.

Follow up soon after the meeting, while staff still remember the stated goals for the site. Have team members visit staff individually to corroborate information, gather new ideas, and explain things in detail.

Educating the Staff

Staff will support the project more if they understand not only the project goals but also the technology surrounding it. If at all possible, offer Internet training sessions for your staff. Objections and hesitation about your library web site will arise because of a simple lack of understanding about the Internet and the World Wide Web. We have found that the more the World Wide Web is understood and used by librarians, the more excited they become about their library's site and the more they have to contribute to it.

Many sessions can be planned and offered concurrently with the development of the home page, and these sessions will be effective if team members offer the training. They can offer glimpses of the work in progress, firsthand instruction about the work they are doing, and assistance to other librarians in using these tools with a focus on library-related content.

Staff benefit greatly by further training on all aspects of the Internet. Start with instruction on basic Internet navigation, and then offer instruction on the specific browsers your library uses. Eventually you should teach HTML authoring to those interested. This will also help to increase the number of staff willing and able to participate in the overall maintenance of the site. At the end of this chapter appears a sample training schedule which illustrates the topics that are relevant when training staff in Internet and World Wide Web use.

Staff should also be given access to equipment on which to experiment with the technology beyond training and workshop times. Whether Netscape or Mosaic is loaded onto each personal workstation or is available on a communal computer, staff should be able to view the project as it will be presented to the public. They will also need time to practice and explore on their own.

You may wish to let others know the URL, or address, so they can watch the progress being made as the site is created, or you may prefer to wait for an unveiling date. If you let others follow the progress, they can add comments or information throughout the process. We have found that this is valuable in creating staff participation. You might feel more comfortable, however, waiting until some of the rough edges are smoothed out before letting anyone see the page.

Staff Training Outline

These are the skills and objectives that have been identified as necessary for working with the library home page. These sections range from general Internet use to creating WWW documents, and serve as a guideline to the development of training materials and workshops.

COMPONENTS OF TRAINING

Basic Internet Skills:
- A basic understanding of what the Internet is and how it is organized
- Basic netiquette issues and conditions of use
- Foundational tools:
  E-mail, gopher, finger, "talk", telnet, confer, listservs

Introduction to World Wide Web:
- Understanding concepts of hypertext, multimedia, distributed information
- Familiarity with different browsers
  Netscape
  Mosaic
  lynx
- Using browsers on different platforms (Macintosh, Windows, UNIX)
- Using search tools such as Lycos, Open Text, and WebCrawler
- Evaluating Internet resources

HTML Skills:
- Familiarity with HTML tags
- Basic graphics skills
- Familiarity with special features (forms, image maps, tables, etc.)
- Familiarity with HTML standards
- Designing documents for multiple platforms

4 Content: Search and Selection

After determining who will work on your library web site project and establishing a plan for the site, you are ready to start gathering content. Collecting content, and giving it design and organization, is perhaps the most important and the most time-consuming part of web site development. Keep in mind that gathering content and working on the design and organization should be simultaneous tasks. Content will affect the design and organization of the site, and vice versa. If different members of the team work on these two tasks, they should communicate, sharing ideas and reports of their progress.

Select Content for Your Goals and Audience

As mentioned before, the Internet is full of flashy yet content-poor resources. A web project can be so exciting that staff may be overcome by the potential of the technology, and may be tempted to put up as much information as possible. However, it is important to keep in mind the original approach chosen for the web site. The approach will affect the type and amount of content you will collect for the web site. If the site is not useful, not well-organized or appealing in design, both staff and patrons may become alienated rather than excited by the project. Below are several pitfalls to avoid, as well as tips for ensuring the success of the content-gathering process.

Do not try to include every piece of information about your library in the first version of your web site. Even if you have decided to produce a more complex web site, it is important that the result is not too overwhelming. Not every detail of the library's operations needs to appear on your web site; select only those details which are interesting to your patrons or staff, and which can be adapted well for the WWW platform. Prioritize content selection to match the goals and needs of your audience. If you try to do too much too fast, the results could be very discouraging. Pages should also be balanced between appealing design and important content.

Do not promise what you cannot support. This is where the level of service to be provided by your web site becomes very important. The content you select should support the goals of the approach originally chosen. If you do not have the staff and time required to support collection development of Internet resources, then do not offer such a service on your web site. If you begin an online resources collection without keeping it up to date and relevant to your patrons' needs, the collection becomes useless. If staff and patrons see that you make promises for services you cannot support, they may lose faith in the project altogether.

Do include library staff in the content-gathering process. Ask staff to contribute ideas for content. If appropriate to your approach and library situation, try to include some kind of information from every department or unit. You may even want to invite staff not directly involved in the project to write or organize different content areas. Including staff in the content-gathering process benefits the project in many ways. Inclusion helps staff feel ownership of the project, stimulates interest in project maintenance, and keeps the web site from becoming too entrenched in one point of view.

Do include a variety of information. A home page or web site that lists only the library hours and policies will not be very useful or interesting. No matter what level of service you have selected, a variety of information can be included. If you have decided to create a basic information page, you will, of course, want to list library hours and contact information, but why not also consider asking the library staff to recommend their favorite books or videos? Be creative no matter what the level of service your web site offers.

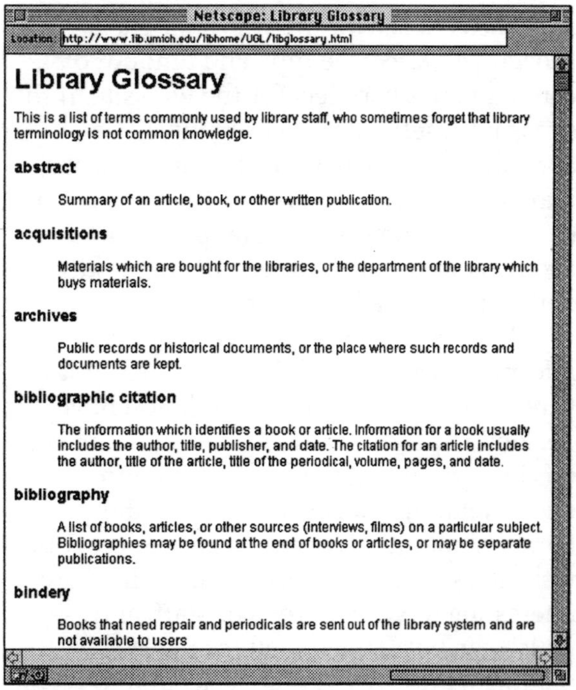
Netscape: Library Glossary

Location: http://www.lib.umich.edu/libhome/UGL/libglossary.html

Library Glossary

This is a list of terms commonly used by library staff, who sometimes forget that library terminology is not common knowledge.

abstract

Summary of an article, book, or other written publication.

acquisitions

Materials which are bought for the libraries, or the department of the library which buys materials.

archives

Public records or historical documents, or the place where such records and documents are kept.

bibliographic citation

The information which identifies a book or article. Information for a book usually includes the author, title, publisher, and date. The citation for an article includes the author, title of the article, title of the periodical, volume, pages, and date.

bibliography

A list of books, articles, or other sources (interviews, films) on a particular subject. Bibliographies may be found at the end of books or articles, or may be separate publications.

bindery

Books that need repair and periodicals are sent out of the library system and are not available to users

FIGURE 4.1
The University of Michigan's glossary of library terms, a handout for patrons adapted for online use

Sources of Content

Now that you have some guidelines for gathering content for your web site, the next step is to actually collect the information. In this section we will discuss what kinds of existing information can be adapted for the online environment, what kinds of new content can be created, and how multimedia resources might be included.

The first place to look to for content is existing print materials. The first source for content could be publications produced by your library, such as any type of material used for library publicity or promotion. Look at handouts developed for patrons (Figure 4.1), library newsletters, press releases, library manuals, handbooks, annual reports, and special publications. Materials you already have in digital format may be especially convenient starting points. Employing an HTML editor can be very useful here, as your text files can be opened in the editor, and the tags can easily be added.

However, several things should be considered before using these materials for web site content. First, almost certainly these materials will need adaptation for online use. Reading a brochure or report in print differs from reading documents online. Most print materials are too lengthy to be directly reproduced as a WWW document. Patrons find long paragraphs of text from a computer screen difficult and boring to read. Think about abridging reports and other lengthy publications for online distribution. You may also want to break up text into smaller documents and add graphics for a more appealing look. In Chapter 5, we will be talking about these kinds of design issues in more depth.

As an aside, examining existing library publications for use on a web site provides a good opportunity to update information. Also, as you adapt print information to WWW documents, you may want to consider dropping some print versions altogether. If you can offer printing from workstations, why not let patrons and staff decide when they need the information in print or when it can be effectively used online?

Many resources, such as a staff directory, can be enriched by moving them to an online format. On paper, a staff directory most likely lists names, telephone numbers, and addresses. As a WWW document, a staff directory can include not only this information, but pictures and links to other documents as well (Figure 4.2). For example, at the University of Michigan, library staff entries are linked to the home pages of the libraries or units within which they work. Pictures are best left optional, but can be very helpful for patrons who may want to connect a specialty or position with a face. They can lend a more human feel to your web site.

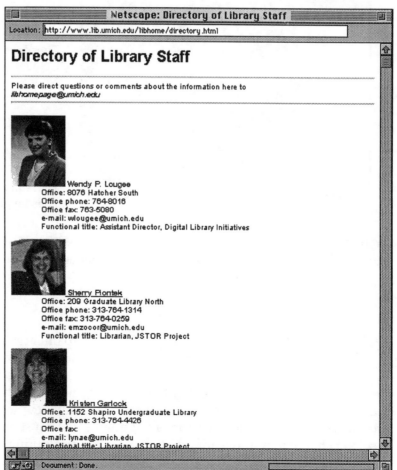

FIGURE 4.2
A staff directory with pictures puts a more human face on a web site.

Fall Internet Workshops

Take advantage of the free Internet workshops offered at the Main Library and Westacres Branch! Below is a list of Beginning Internet workshops which cover basic gopher browsing and Veronica searching. Anyone who attends a beginning workshop is automatically added to our mailing list and will receive notices of advanced workshops (held at the Main Library).

Registration for classes begins 7 days prior to the date of class. You must be a resident of West Bloomfield, Commerce Township, Keego Harbor, Orchard Lake, or Sylvan Lake to participate.

An Internet class at the Westacres Branch

MAIN LIBRARY--ADULT WORKSHOPS
(Ages 16 years and up / limited to 10)
Monday, October 9, 7:00 - 8:00 p.m.
Wednesday, October 11, 7:00 - 8:00 p.m.
Tuesday, October 17, 7:00 - 8:00 p.m.
Monday, October 23, 7:00 - 8:00 p.m.
Wednesday, October 25, 7:00 - 8:00 p.m.
Tuesday, October 31, 7:00 - 8:00 p.m.
Tuesday, November 7, 7:00 - 8:00 p.m.
Monday, November 13, 7:00 - 8:00 p.m.
Wednesday, November 15, 7:00 - 8:00 p.m.
Tuesday, November 21, 7:00 - 8:00 p.m.
Monday, November 27, 7:00 - 8:00 p.m.
Wednesday, November 29, 7:00 - 8:00 p.m.
Tuesday, December 5, 7:00 - 8:00 p.m.
Monday, December 11, 7:00 - 8:00 p.m.
Wednesday, December 13, 7:00 - 8:00 p.m.

MAIN LIBRARY--YOUTH WORKSHOPS
(Ages 10 - 15 / limited to 6)
Thursday, September 21, 7:00 - 8:00 p.m.
Saturday, September 30, 10:00 - 11:00 a.m.
Thursday, October 19, 7:00 - 8:00 p.m.
Saturday, November 4, 10:00 - 11:00 a.m.
Thursday, December 7, 7:00 - 8:00 p.m.

WESTACRES--ADULT WORKSHOPS
(Ages 16 years and up / limited to 6)
Tuesdays, 10:30 - 11:30 a.m.
October 3, 24, 31
November 7, 14, 21, 28
December 5, 12

WESTACRES--YOUTH WORKSHOPS
(Ages 10 - 15 / limited to 6)
Wednesday, September 27, 4:00 - 5:00 p.m.
Tuesday, October 17, 4:00 - 5:00 p.m.
Thursday, November 9, 4:00 - 5:00 p.m.
Tuesday, December 5, 4:00 - 5:00 p.m.

FIGURE 4.3
Library-sponsored computing workshops may help introduce your new site to the community.

Creating New Content

An important part of the content-gathering process will be creating new content for the project. View the web site development as an excellent chance to improve information which you offer library staff and patrons, and to offer new types of information resources which were not possible to offer in print.

Start by examining what might be new about your library. Have you added any new services lately? Perhaps you have just recently developed a set of computing workshops for library patrons (Figure 4.3).

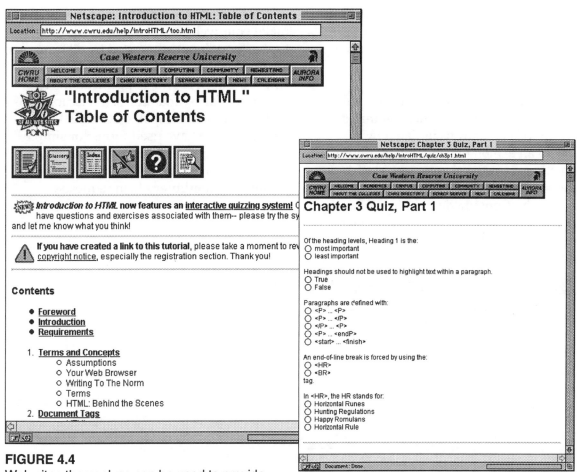

FIGURE 4.4
Web sites themselves can be used to provide computing tutorials.

In addition to announcing the workshops on the library web site, workshop materials and online tutorials can be made available. If you have created any kind of slides or overhead images for your workshops in a digital format, they can be easily converted to image files or HTML files. You may even consider creating an original WWW presentation. A WWW presentation can include links to resources which you may want to demonstrate. Instead of flipping between a WWW browser and overheads, why not make your presentation outline an HTML document and embed the links within it? For a great example of this type of presentation, see Figure 4.4.

New acquisitions also offer great potential as web site content. Traditional means of showcasing new materials are "new book"

areas, printed lists, and special labels, but the Web adds a new facet to publicizing new materials. Put up a list of new materials, but add some value to it by including some special links to information about certain materials. For example, if you have acquired a new book by Anne Rice, you could include information about the Anne Rice USENET discussion group, **alt.books.anne-rice**. Asking staff members or patrons to offer reviews and recommendations of books, videos, and Internet resources is another good idea (Figure 4.5). These promotional techniques need not be limited to new materials only. They work just as well for recommending other holdings.

Have you hosted any special events lately? WWW technology is especially suited to displaying information about such events, and listing upcoming events. You can include pictures, text from speeches, or a list of further readings related to a program, among many other things (Figure 4.6).

Is your library expanding or being renovated? You may want to consider making floor plans available online. You might even want to keep patrons updated by putting up an exhibit of construction photos. During a long construction project, staff and patrons sometimes find it hard to believe an end is in sight. Construction photos not only mark progress, but also serve as an archival record of the project (Figure 4.7).

You can even use WWW technology to make your web site interactive. Fill-out forms, though not supported by all browsers, are great features which you may choose to employ. Check browser specifications to determine form capabilities. (Netscape, lynx, and Mosaic are all capable of forms.) Libraries on the Web have used forms for simple feedback, interfaces to online catalogs (see Chapter 1), and even as mechanisms for submitting interlibrary loan requests (Figure 4.8).

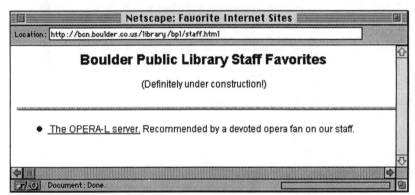

FIGURE 4.5
Materials promotion efforts may include new acquisitions, reviews and recommendations, or even staff recommendations of favorite Internet sites.

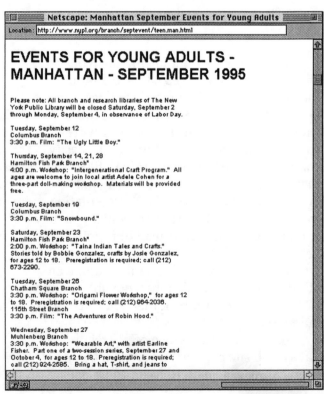

FIGURE 4.6
A listing of library events from the New York Public Library home page

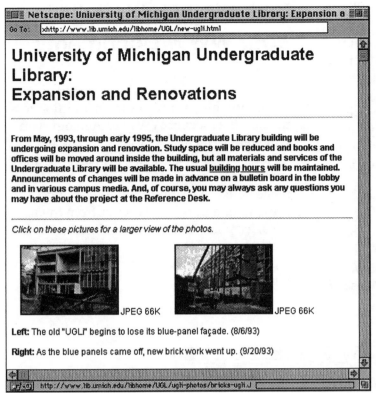

FIGURE 4.7
Pictures of library construction projects help keep patrons updated on progress while also creating an archival record of the work.

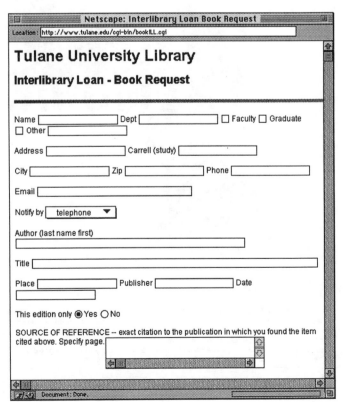

FIGURE 4.8
An interactive form allowing patrons to make interlibrary loan requests

For learning about forms, see the fill-out forms portion of the Web Communications HTML Tutorial (**http://www.webcom.com/~webcom/html/tutor/forms/**). Fill-out forms are relatively easy to create. The form interface is constructed by using HTML tags. However, to activate your forms, you will need to have a program available on your server to send your form to its desired destination. This program is generally called a "script" and will most likely be UNIX-based. The script will need to configured on your server by a system administrator. For more technical information about forms and the scripts they require, take a look at the Fill-Out Forms Overview from NCSA (**http://www.ncsa.uiuc.edu/SDG/Software/Mosaic/Docs/fill-out-forms/overview.html**).

Including Multimedia in Your WWW Documents

Multimedia content should be included in some form on your web site. In addition to making the most of WWW technology, you will want to include graphics and other media in your documents, primarily because some people are visually oriented—they relate better to graphical interfaces and presentations, and learn better from them. Also, graphics and other multimedia features make documents more attractive and appealing, especially to younger patrons (Figure 4.9).

FIGURE 4.9
Multimedia content increases a web site's appeal, particularly for younger viewers.

FIGURE 4.10
A letterhead logo such as
these examples can make
your web site readily
recognizable as an official
library resource.

Using Library Logos

Recognizable library logos should be incorporated in your web identity. If you have a special header on letterhead, you may want to modify it for use on your WWW documents. Patrons will see this header or logo, and recognize the document as an official library resource (Figure 4.10).

In addition to graphics, WWW documents can include video clips and sound. Most video clips should be kept short; even short clips can be very large in size and take a long time to load. Video clips can be employed as "teasers" for other resources or programs. Video clips require either converting a regular video clip to a digital video format, or using a digital video camera to create the clip (Figure 4.11).

Sound can also be added to WWW documents. You might like to include a welcome message from your director as the St. Joseph County Public Library does (Figure 4.12).

Accessing both video clips and sound files requires external software applications.

A popular application for viewing video clips is Sparkle, while Sound Machine is often used to listen to sound files. Generally, these helper applications are included in the network browser package. Appendix A includes a list of resources on adding multimedia to your WWW documents.

These examples provide just a few exciting ideas for local content that can be modified from existing library information or newly created. The World Wide Web allows available print materials to appear in a new format, and expands the possible types of information available to patrons. Multimedia not only breaks up the monotony of textual documents for all patrons, but appeals to visually oriented patrons.

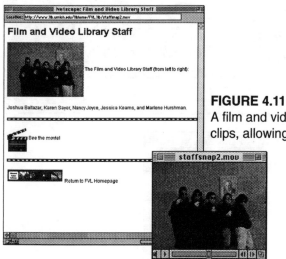

FIGURE 4.11
A film and video library site incorporates video clips, allowing patrons to see a brief movie.

FIGURE 4.12
This introductory message is both seen and heard.

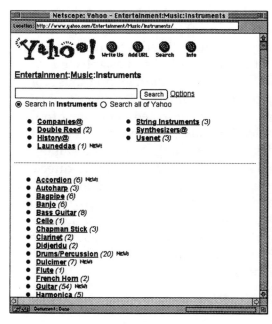

FIGURE 4.13
Subject directories make browsing for nonspecific Internet resources easy, but do not offer consistency in their classification schemes.

Including Remote Content

While locally produced content offers the advantage of easier control, maintenance, and evaluation, many valuable Internet resources exist which can enrich your library collection and become important information resources for your patrons. If you decide to include an Internet resources collection, you must first locate, and then evaluate, the resources.

Finding Remote Resources

Two of the most valuable tools for creating an Internet resources collection for your web site are subject catalogs or directories, and search engines. As you are aware, no "official" guidelines exist regarding the creation of WWW documents. However, "de facto" standards have developed as Internet users have come to realize the need for some sort of consistency on which subject directories and search engines must depend.

Subject directories offer the best starting point when browsing for Internet resources

without a specific resource in mind. Search engines, which are databases of links to Internet documents, offer different kinds of searching mechanisms and are best used when you have a specific resource or search term in mind. Because of their popularity, the best search engines sometimes get overloaded with requests, while subject directories are much more accessible. A list of some recommended subject directories and search engines appears at the end of this chapter.

Subject Directories

Besides subject directories' ease of access, they offer several other advantages. The most popular and well-established subject directories generally include primary Internet resources on any given topic. If you have only a vague idea of what you seek, browsing a subject directory provides ideas for more specific terminology and searches. Most subject directories also include resources in many different Internet formats, including gophers, FTP sites, and WWW resources (Figure 4.13).

One should keep in mind a few things when using subject directories. First, there is no complete and official catalog of Internet resources—all subject directories are created and maintained by independent individuals or organizations. No uniform vocabulary exists—each directory creator uses nonstandard subject headings, which might make a natural language search approach easier, but guarantees no consistency between different directories. Some organizations, however, are using standard library classification schemes to create subject catalogs of Internet resources. The WWW Virtual Library has one such project in the works using the Library of Congress classification scheme (Figure 4.14).

Using a variety of subject directories helps when browsing for Internet resources. In addition to using different terminologies, individual subject directories also cover different resources. While many subject directories do not include evaluative information about their listed resources, some do. One of the most useful and established subject directories is the Clearinghouse for Subject-Oriented Internet Resource Guides (**http://www.lib.umich.edu/chhome.html**). The Clearinghouse, a collection of Internet guides on certain subjects, offers a value-added approach to topical resource directories (Figure 4.15). The guides, created by individuals all over the world, provide more than just lists of sites; the majority include evaluative information about resources, with comments sometimes tailored to specific audiences.

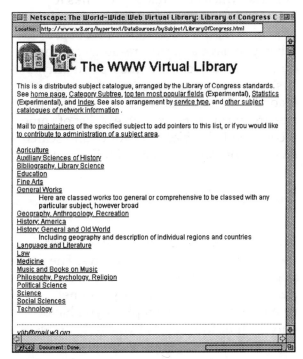

FIGURE 4.14
The WWW Virtual Library, which uses the Library of Congress classification scheme

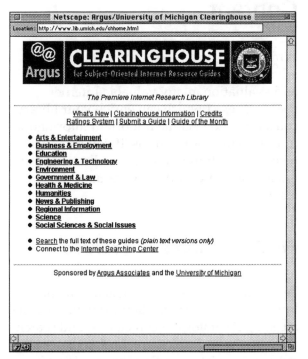

FIGURE 4.15
The Clearinghouse for Subject-Oriented Internet Resource Guides offers a subject directory that provides evaluative information about Internet sites.

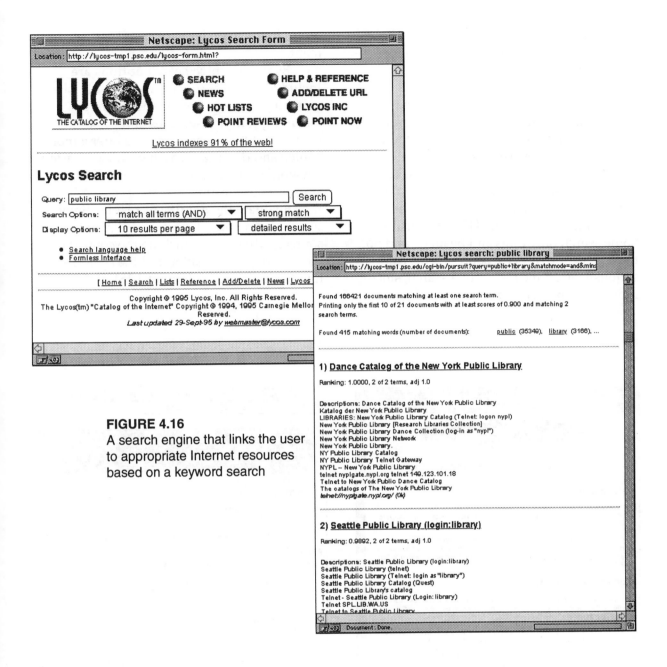

FIGURE 4.16
A search engine that links the user to appropriate Internet resources based on a keyword search

Search Engines

Search engines, an alternative tool for compiling a collection of Internet resources, are becoming more comprehensive, accessible, and reliable all the time. Search engines often utilize the HTML forms capability. Searches are entered into appropriate fields, the queries are submitted to the database, and the results displayed include links to the specific resources (Figure 4.16).

Search engines work by searching a database of resource links. Like subject directories, search engines are not comprehensive, but include major Internet resources in many different subject areas. This is why it is important to regularly use a variety of search engines in order to get the best results possible. Familiarize yourself with each search engine to choose the best one for your task.

Evaluate the coverage of the database. The best search engines list the number of resources included in their database and what type of resources are included (gophers, FTP sites, WWW resources, etc.). Some search engines only include WWW resources, and some databases are much more comprehensive than others (Figure 4.17).

Evaluate how the search works. You should note several things about how the search engine functions. Search engines search different parts of HTML documents. Some search only titles and headers, and not the full text of WWW resources. This can seriously affect the results of a search, since more descriptive information can often be found in the main body of an HTML document.

Evaluate which search options are included. Some search engines offer Boolean searching options, even to the extent of including complex searches and proximity operators. Other search engines offer a more "quick and dirty" approach with very basic keyword searching. This too, will affect your approach and results.

Evaluate the display of results. Some search engines display a simple list of resources, while others include the context of the hit, weighted results, and the option to link to similar pages (Figure 4.18).

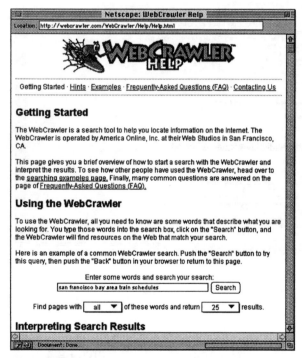

FIGURE 4.17
A basic search engine that provides only a list of resources

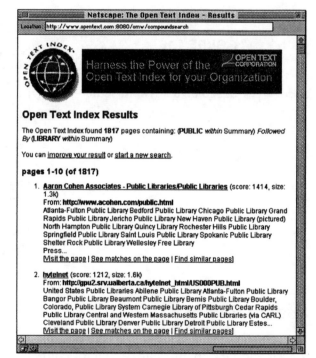

FIGURE 4.18
A more complex search engine that provides weighted results and the option of linking to similar pages

Searching Strategies

The lack of organization within the WWW makes choosing an effective searching strategy difficult. Unlike commercial databases or library catalogs, the Internet offers few chances to use controlled vocabulary in a search. Indexing and subject term assignment often result from the creativity of a resource developer, and so-called subject headings may be more descriptive than consistent. Furthermore, the impossibility of gauging the amount of material that might be retrieved makes tailoring a search difficult. A carefully constructed search might retrieve hundreds of resources, or nothing.

These suggestions can be employed to make searching more productive:

- Before searching, browse through the subject directories discussed above to get an idea about terms commonly used to describe your topic.

- Think of as many keywords as you can—search engines primarily operate using the subject terminology maintainers create, and these are almost always natural language terms.

- Investigate the various search engines and spend some time becoming acquainted with the way they operate. Different tools search different parts of a document, include different documents in their databases, and present results differently.

- Duplicate a search on multiple search engines to increase comprehensiveness. You will probably find entirely different resources in your results when you try a different searching tool.

- Try your search at different times duing the day. During peak business hours connecting to popular searching sites may be difficult.

Evaluating Remote Resources

The World Wide Web contains a wealth of resources, but bear in mind that not all contain accurate information. For the same reasons that print resources need to be judged for quality, WWW resources also require evaluation. Traditional evaluation practices of collection librarians when deciding whether to include a print resource in a collection apply to Internet resource collection as well.

For example, these suggestions for evaluating Internet resources may parallel considerations that apply to print resource evaluation:

- What is the intended audience for the resource? Is it intended for an academic audience or for a popular one? How does this compare to your intended audience?

- How frequently is the resource updated and reviewed? Reputable sources tend to have a date affixed indicating that the resource was updated recently.

- Is there an affiliated institution? Is it academic or commercial? Commercial organizations have some excellent resources published on the WWW, but might have a different point of view than an academic or personal source.

- What is the resource developer's expertise? Is there an "about" section of the document that describes the author/creator?

- What is the relationship between the resource and other similar or dissimilar resources about the same topic? Does it contain links to other resources, or does it contribute original information? It may be useful to include a resource with links to other sites if they are unique to your collection, or you may want to include only sites that contribute unique information.

- What do others with the same interests think of the site? Is the site reviewed or evalutaed anywhere? Reputation counts for a lot on the Internet.

- Are there any special requirements for using this resource? For example, does it require access permissions? If your audience cannot access a resource without obtaining passwords, it might not be a useful resource to include in your collection.

Once you have selected local and remote resources for inclusion in your web site, the next step will be to display this content in an appealing manner. Chapter Five offers strategies for organizing content and using HTML tagging and multimedia to create both useful and attractive WWW documents.

A List of Subject Directories and Search Engines

Subject Directories

- **Clearinghouse for Subject-Oriented Internet Resource Guides**

  (http://http2.sils.umich.edu/~lou/chhome.html)

  The Clearinghouse for Subject-Oriented Internet Resource Guides is a collection of subject-based guides which offer evaluative information about Internet resources. The guides cover subjects from neuroscience to library employment, and are available in text and/or HTML format.

- **WWW Virtual Library**

  (http://www.w3.org/hypertext/DataSources/bySubject/Overview.html)

  The WWW Virtual Library is a collection of WWW documents, compiled from requests sent to **www-request@info.cern.ch** and other sites. Exploring the catalog of resources by Library of Congress subject headings (experimental) and geographic location are also options. A list of additional virtual libraries is available.

- **Yahoo**

  (http://www.yahoo.com/)

  Yahoo, with thousands of items in its catalog, is one of the most comprehensive subject directories of Internet resources. In addition to browsing, the Yahoo catalog allows you to search its collection, add new resources, and has its own "What's New" and "Random Link" features.

Search Engines

- **Lycos**

  (http://lycos.cs.cmu.edu/)

  Lycos, once provided by Carnegie-Mellon University, is now known as Lycos, Inc. Lycos searches titles, headings, links, and keywords. Lycos also provides a browsing feature, and includes more than 1 million sites in its catalog. Lycos offers search results with title, outline, keywords and an excerpt that provides some context.

- **Open Text Web Index**

  (http://opentext.uunet.ca:8080/)

  The Web index provided by the Open Text Corporation, a software company based in Canada, allows searches on full text or within specified document fields. The index offers a choice between a simple search or a power search; the form for the power search offers Boolean and proximity options. It retrieves information quickly, and provides the number of retrieved documents in sets of ten.

- **WebCrawler**

  (http://www.webcrawler.com)

  WebCrawler, which allows searches by document title and content, offers a form interface that allows the Boolean "and" as well as a simple search page. It works well for general, "quick and dirty" searches, and is usually not as busy as some of other sites.

5 Presentation: Style and Structure

You may find, at this point, that you have a lot of material and no idea how to organize it. You also want your site to be as attractive as possible. On a web site, design and organization are intertwined, and this chapter gives you some guidelines to help you achieve the best of both.

Taking first things first, look at what you will be working with: your audience, the current web situation around you, and the distinctive characteristics of the web as a medium. These things cannot be changed, so you need to work with them for the best results.

Your audience is why you are creating the site in the first place. While you hope to attract a larger audience for your web page eventually, you need to think about who your initial audience will be. Remember to design for this audience; the site you personally like might not be a resource your current audience will find useful. Ponder the impression you want to create, and then compare it to the impression that would best suit the audience you have identified as yours.

If you work in an academic institution, you might determine that a formal tone suits your audience best. Or if you serve a smaller body of users within a larger academic institution, you might want to adopt a style tailored for them. The Shapiro Undergraduate Library at the University of Michigan, for instance, although part of the larger University Library, has taken a lighter tone than some of the more research-oriented libraries in the system. Its undergraduate constituency generally makes this lighter approach more appropriate (Figure 5.1).

Those of you at a public or school library will want to examine the community you serve when deciding upon the impression you are striving for. The writing style you use, as well as the resources you offer, will depend on your users. Remember to use the language and vocabulary of your audience (Figure 5.2).

You must also work with the web situation around you, whatever it might be. Your page might be part of a larger institutional web site, in which case the style of writing, the graphics used, and the links included may have to complement existing work. If, on the other hand, you start an independent site, you will have more freedom to experiment with design and style.

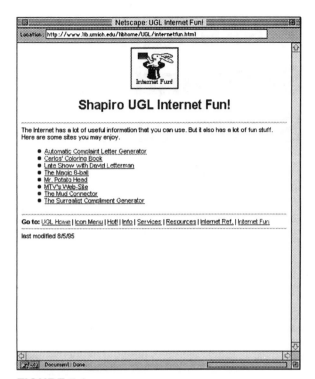

FIGURE 5.1
This undergraduate library web site targets its audience with an appropriately light, informal tone.

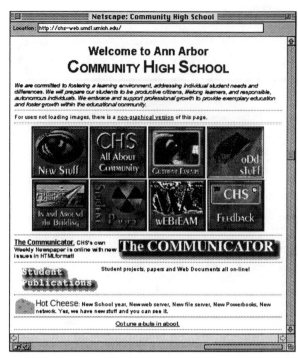

FIGURE 5.2
A web site should speak in the vocabulary of its constituents, as shown by this high school's home page

Finally, your organization and design are dependent on the characteristics of hypertext. You want to use this hypertextual capability to your advantage, to make the most of the way the Web works. Unlike other media that you may have used to promote your library in the past, such as print or video, the web is flexible, malleable, and interactive. Whatever you put up can easily be changed, so your site can evolve with your library. Patron suggestions can be considered and implemented immediately. This flexibility makes web design more dynamic than previous forms of promotion, but calls for new design principles that will inform the way you structure your site.

Web Space Structure

The use of hypertext lets you create a web-like information system, with unique navigational possibilities. At any point you can give your users multiple choices, let them move back and forth, or guide them through an intuitive informational path (Figure 5.3). This interactive approach has much more impact than a linear print or video presentation of the same information. Users can move in any direction depending on what they choose to view next, while you can control the choices offered by the links you create. In fact, many library classes and tutorials are now offered

FIGURE 5.3
An interactive home page that incorporates hypertext, allowing users to choose navigational options

FIGURE 5.4
A diagram helps establish logical connections when mapping out a new web site.

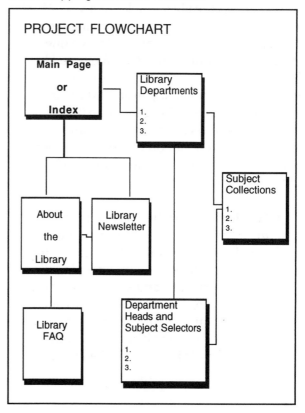

on the Web because of the ease of guiding users through a path of options.

On the other hand, all of the possibilities hypertext presents can make the job of creating a web site confusing. You may encounter difficulty in sorting out and keeping track of links that should follow each other logically. In the beginning stages of designing a web site, a good way to spot connections and develop a logical structure is to create a story board or flowchart that maps out your intended site. Doing it on paper or on a blackboard will help you discover the places where connections exist and where links should be made. You will save a lot of time if this structure is prepared before tagging begins (Figure 5.4).

Remember to make your links practical, logical, and consistent. Think of the obvious ones—a description of a subject collection linked to the special librarian for that area, a library collection linked to its location on a map, a special collections library linked to an exhibit—and then move on to more advanced connections, such as outside resources and new resources developed within your own library. A note of caution: first-time web designers often insert links and create multiple layers simply because they can, but you should not bury basic, important information too deeply. Users can get lost or frustrated looking for what they need. The means of obtaining basic information should be obvious.

Adapting Content

After setting up a basic structure, you need to take a second look at the information and data already gathered and decide if this information is really suitable for a WWW presentation. You may need to change the format or edit the style or length. No one particularly wants to use the Web to read long text files. If you include information currently in handouts, you should consider rewriting them, breaking them up into smaller linked sections, or using some graphical representation of the information. As you evaluate which information to include, ask yourself:

- Would this work best as one long document, or should it be divided into smaller sections linked together? If the page has information that people will want to print out and save, present it as one long page so that it can be printed out as a complete document. If it contains information about several different topics, divide it up into linked sections.

- Are there aspects of the content that could lend themselves to a multimedia format? Would graphics portray the information better? Images often convey information much more quickly and effectively than text.

- Is this information written in the style and with the vocabulary that web-users (particularly your local audience) will find interesting?

Document Style

All of the pages within your site should share a similar design and style so that users will recognize them as belonging to your library. This requires consistency not only in the graphics used, but in the overall structure of the pages and writing style of the documents. To ensure similarity among pages, design a template to serve as a useful guide for the various team members working on the site. The template ensures that basic information, such as contact persons and location, will not be overlooked, and guides the team in the formatting of a document. Those working on different areas of the site can add to or modify this template. The template does not have to be an ironclad set of tags, but it should be followed at least minimally to maintain a consistency of style and look.

A template also ensures that each page within the site is a complete presentation. While all sections and subsections of the site should fit together logically, each page should be able to stand on its own, identifying the library and letting the users know exactly what they are looking at. Even on pages that do no more than provide links to other sources, the nature and subject area of those links should be obvious.

As for writing style, make sure the writing is well done, just as you would with any of your library's materials. Go for a

FIGURE 5.5
A common road sign on the information superhighway

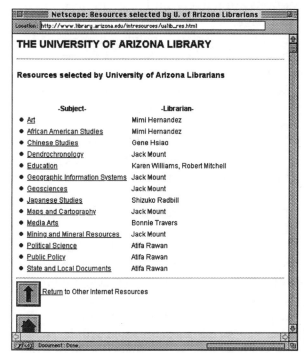

FIGURE 5.6
An organizational scheme for presenting
both local and remote resources

classic style which avoids clumsy or cute phrases. You should particularly avoid overused Internet jargon like CLICK HERE! (context and highlighting should make it obvious where to click) or UNDER CONSTRUCTION! It's assumed that all pages are "under construction," and yours should be, too (Figure 5.5). Just as you are always creating new print documentation to match changes in users and in resources, you should be prepared to change your online presentation as well. Your writing style, though, should be consistently well done, regardless of changes made in design or content.

Organizing Resources

Whether you include local or remote resources, you will want to establish an organizational scheme for presenting these resources. Some libraries move the Dewey Decimal system over to their web resources, while others create their own schemes. Whichever route you choose, your primary audience should be the main consideration as you label these resources (Figure 5.6).

Remember that your site will expand and change over time. Avoid creating a structure with dead ends—assume that your collections will get larger, and that relevant resources on the Web will increase. Using a logical organizational structure from the beginning makes things much simpler as your collection of resources expands.

Visual Design

While the structure and organization of your site are critical, the look and feel of your site also affects users' impression of your work. The appearance of the site depends not only on your use of images and graphics, but also on the navigational icons, arrangement of text, and use of typographical styles.

Even if you lack technical knowledge of graphic design, you will want to use graphics to enhance the presentation of information. Thoughtful use of images enhances the site and makes it easier for users to navigate. Graphics can be used as headers (mastheads, seals, or photos of your library); navigational icons ("Go," "Back," "Home"); illustrations to supplement text (maps, floor plans); and as images which have been ismapped, that is, on which hypertext links have been created within the image.

Navigational icons, if used, should be unobtrusive but their meaning obvious

(Figure 5.7). They should appear in a consistent manner on every page of the web site, so avoid colors or designs that will detract from the unique content of each page. Steer away from icons that are ubiquitous—there are too many little houses being used to signify "home"—and find something unique. Placing a single, slim toolbar at the bottom or top of each page, rather than many separate icons, reiterates navigational options attractively, and takes up less space on a page.

Floor plans and shelving diagrams of libraries are easily created, and they can convey directional information much more effectively than wordy instructions (Figure 5.8). Other maps can be used where appropriate.

The use of ismapped images, or image-mapping, is an especially effective technique. Sections of images can be made to act as hypertext links, enabling users to click on images rather than text to move to another document (Figure 5.9).

Learning how to create digital images requires some training, but a lot can be done with basic software packages designed for drawing, painting, and manipulating images. By experimenting with these readily available packages you will learn quickly how they work. Investing in one of these packages before starting the project would be a wise choice if you think you will

FIGURE 5.7
A toolbar of navigational icons

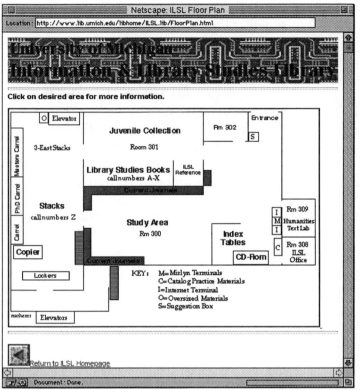

FIGURE 5.8
A floor plan provides directional information more effectively than a written description.

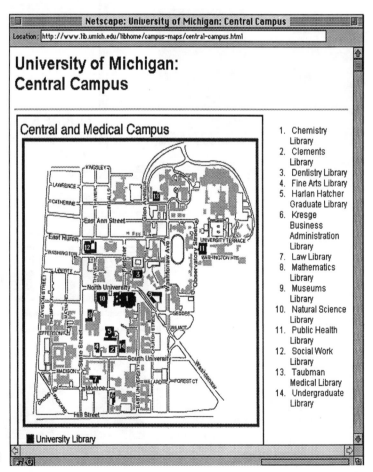

FIGURE 5.9
An ismapped image

be creating any of your own images. We have mentioned sites on the web that make images and icons available (Appendix A); with imaging software you can use these images and also adapt their size, color, or shape, to fit the design of your site.

Photographs converted to a digital format can also be included. Conversion involves scanning already existing prints or slides. New images may be created by using a digital camera. Once again, digitizing photographs requires some experience with the tools, but these skills can be quickly acquired with a small amount of practice.

When using images on web pages, whether they have been created or acquired, keep in mind some basic principles:

- If your page has links to external images, provide a description and the size of the image next to the link. This permits users to decide if they really want to wait for the image to load (Figure 5.10). Or, alternatively, provide a smaller thumbnail version of the image as a preview of the larger image, again with file size and description (Figure 5.11).

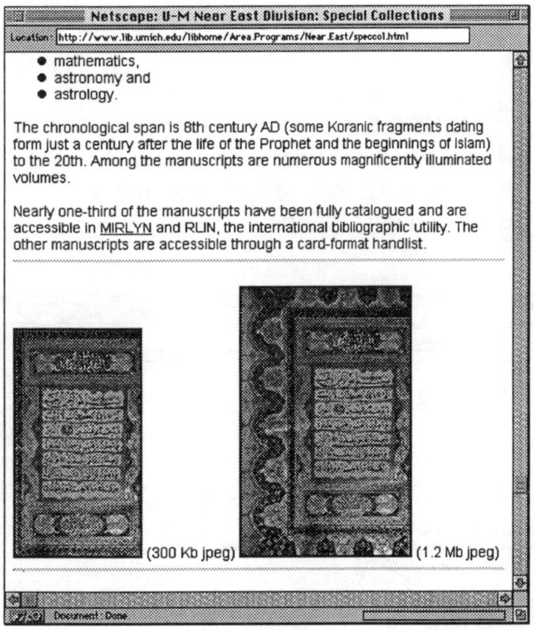

FIGURE 5.10
Sizes given beside images indicate to the user whether a larger version of the image will take long to load.

FIGURE 5.11
A thumbnail serves as a preview of a larger, slower loading image.

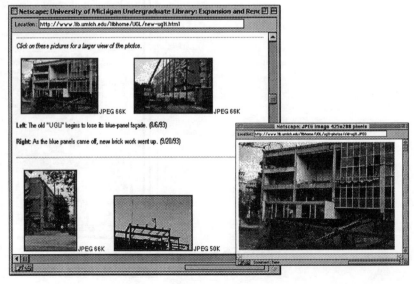

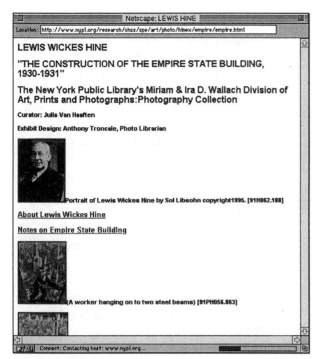

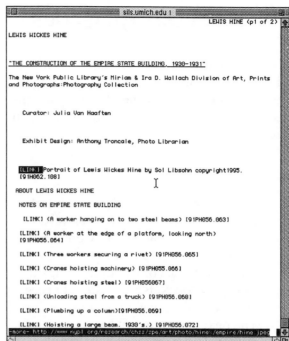

FIGURE 5.12
Some browsers can display images, while others display only text

- Do not use a lot of images on any one page. Again, more images require more time to appear on the browser, and viewing a lot of images with little accompanying content may annoy users.

- Remember that not all browsers show images. As a courtesy to those unable to view images, use alternative text (the <alt> tag) so they, too, can see the information contained in the image (Figure 5.12).

The way you break up your text will also affect the way your page looks. HTML offers limited options for text placement and formatting, so you will have to experiment with tagging. After arranging text and images on a page, have others on the team check for an overall impression. Tell them to look for:

- too much text blocked together without a break, heading, or image

- overdone styles, such as too many bold or emphatic phrases, or too many headers

- too many links next to each other

- links made up of too many words (this creates a "wall of blue")

- lengthy textual descriptions of things that could be best handled with images

Try new approaches and experiment with new styles, but do not let the design detract from the message. Let there be a practical reason for every choice you make.

Practical Design Issues

Even if you do not feel especially confident about your design capabilities, following some common sense principles will guarantee a pleasing web site. Keep in mind as you work:

- You will want to check your work on different browsers as you progress because they all have different interfaces and present tagged text differently. Do not design the page for any one browser, but rather develop a design that works on all of them. For example, things that look good on Netscape will not necessarily translate well to lynx or Mosaic. The next generation of browsers might render your pages completely differently, so keep checking as new software emerges.

- On the same note, do not overuse tags created to work on only one browser. Certain HTML tags are part of the evolving standard and are compatible with the majority of browsers, while other tags were created and are usable only for a specific browser. They may enable some attractive features such as colorful backgrounds, different font-sizing, or more advanced formatting, but if you use too many of them you may be overlooking some of your users.

- Also remember that backgrounds will give the page a "poster" effect. This may be useful as a special highlight, but a plain background works better if you want to present information that requires sustained attention.

- When you view your work in progress, examine it in a text-only browser, such as lynx. When you do this, it becomes obvious if you have too many images and not enough content. It will make you aware of how much concrete information is actually being conveyed on your pages, and how much is filler.

- If you link to information at another site, say so. You should also provide some comments or annotation about the site being linked to. Let users know that they are leaving your site for another, and let them know why.

- Make sure all of the links work and avoid the embarrassment of having links that go nowhere. Links might not work because of a typing error in the URL or in the tagging, or because an address might have changed. To help keep up with these possible changes or errors, have other team members check your work, or designate one person to go through and check links periodically, or investigate using an automated link-checker to make the work easier. The next chapter on maintenance discusses link-checkers in more detail; basically they are programs written to test your links and verify that they still work. Programs such as these require some technical knowledge. If you decide to use them, you should run them regularly to keep your page up to date.

- Check your spelling and grammar carefully—sloppiness really affects the overall presentation and reflects poorly upon your library. Run documents through the spell-checker of a word processor or have someone else proofread for you. Print out your pages so that you can proofread the text on paper. This method is better for finding mistakes than reading from a computer screen.

- Make contact information easy to find. Affix the date and sign each page with your name and e-mail address, especially when it has been updated or changed. This informs users of the currency of the information and makes it easy for them to give feedback and responses.

- Put the URL on your page for those who might want to print it out. Browsers do not add the address of a document to the printed page, and your users consider the address of your site an important piece of information, especially if they take the time to save the document (Figure 5:13).

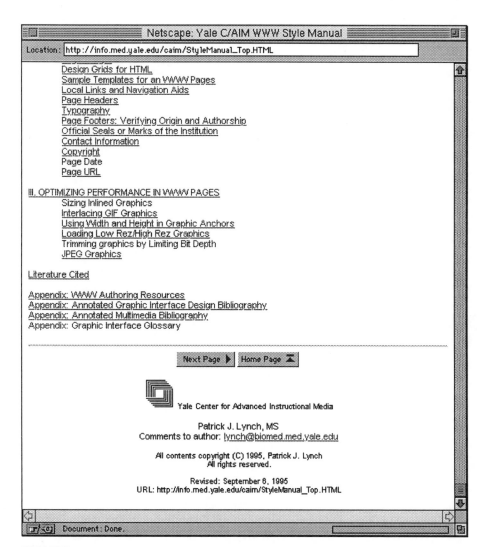

FIGURE 5.13

A good home page shows your name and e-mail address, the date on which the page was last revised, and the address of the site.

- The title of each page within your web site should have enough information in it to identify your library. For example, the title "Circulation" could refer to any library in the world; "University of Michigan University Library: Circulation Services" leaves no doubt in anyone's mind which library is being referred to.

- If you use fill-out forms, make sure to ask questions that will elicit the information you want to receive. Do not ask open-ended questions if you want specific answers. For example, when seeking book purchase suggestions, do not ask for "Information about the item." Ask for "Author's Last Name," "Author's First Name," "ISBN," and so on.

Remember, the simplest presentation often provides information best. Users who access your page often will tire quickly of large images and trendy effects. The best rule of thumb for web design is to make sure that your content is useful, abundant, and well organized.

6 The Dynamic Web Site: Promotion, Evaluation and Maintenance

By now you probably realize that your web site will never be completely finished. As you promote your site, get feedback from your users, and discover new resources and ideas, you will continually be adding to and rearranging your site and its design. These ongoing activities of promotion, evaluation and maintenance will be intertwined as the site emerges. Promotional activities will influence the audience and the feedback received from them, and maintenance activities will be determined by these changes. In this chapter we discuss each of these components—promotion, evaluation and maintenance—and how they interact. Understand that they all depend on each other; none takes place independently, and all play a part in the success of a site.

Attracting Visitors

As with any new service or product, you will want to let people know about your site so they will use it. You want patrons to know that your library is keeping up with Internet technology and the possibilities the technology offers. There is no more effective way to do this than to advertise that you have a WWW site. If you have seen the business cards of other librarians with their web site addresses, or received e-mail with a URL included with the signature, you know that these both are simple, but obvious, means of promoting a site, and they serve as reminders that this business is becoming more common all the time.

When beginning promotion, consider where and how to publicize the page for the best results. As you think about where to start, remember that you can concentrate your efforts within two main target areas: the local community and the WWW community. The "how" of publicizing will then be tailored to each of these areas.

Realize that when you advertise your site, you promote your library as a whole, and create an image for your library. This image will be projected throughout your local community as well as the Internet community.

Publicizing in Your Local Community

When publicizing your web site within your local community, first decide how much time, effort, and money you want to invest in this publicity. You may choose to use tried-and-true promotional techniques that do not require much time or money, such as publicizing the site in the library newsletter, circulating handouts and flyers (Figure 6.1), or announcing it in the local newspaper.

You may also decide to invest in more elaborate schemes. For example, the official unveiling of the project becomes a special event by combining it with an open house or showcase in the library (Figure 6.2). You could also have a special presentation on a community network television program, or in the local newspaper.

Visit us on the World Wide Web!
http://www.lib.umich.edu/libhome/UGL/uglib.html

Come to the Reference Desk on the main floor if you want help navigating the internet or using Netscape. See over for other helpful library URLs and check out What's Cool & What's New on Netscape for fun.

The University of Michigan
Shapiro Undergraduate Library

This bookmark is printed on acid-free paper. It will not become brittle, nor will it cause deterioration of a book in which it is used.

Internet Public Library **http://ipl.sils.umich.edu/**
Mere words fail to describe it; you *must* look at this on-line library.

U of M Digital Library - links to a variety of electronic resources
http://www.lib.umich.edu/libhome/electres.html
Quick and easy access to the Business and Law libraries, for example.

Electronic Reference Shelf **http://www.umich.edu/refshelf/**
An almanac, a thesaurus, *The Oxford English Dictionary*, & more!

FIGURE 6.1
A bookmark used for publicizing a web site

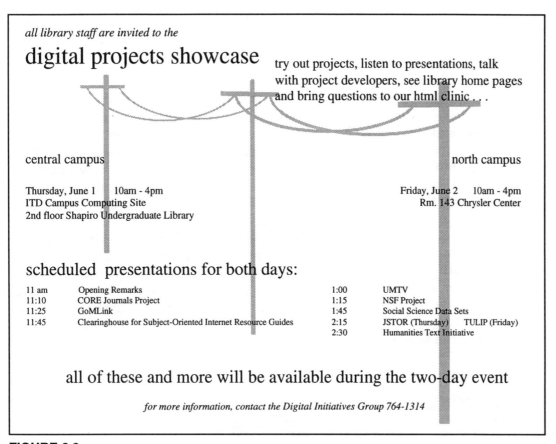

all library staff are invited to the

digital projects showcase

try out projects, listen to presentations, talk with project developers, see library home pages and bring questions to our html clinic . . .

central campus   north campus

Thursday, June 1   10am - 4pm   Friday, June 2   10am - 4pm
ITD Campus Computing Site   Rm. 143 Chrysler Center
2nd floor Shapiro Undergraduate Library

scheduled presentations for both days:

11 am	Opening Remarks	1:00	UMTV
11:10	CORE Journals Project	1:15	NSF Project
11:25	GoMLink	1:45	Social Science Data Sets
11:45	Clearinghouse for Subject-Oriented Internet Resource Guides	2:15	JSTOR (Thursday) TULIP (Friday)
		2:30	Humanities Text Initiative

all of these and more will be available during the two-day event

for more information, contact the Digital Initiatives Group 764-1314

FIGURE 6.2
Promotion of a library web site is included at this special event.

Conducting Workshops

If you decide to go this route, consider the possibility of having a follow-up schedule of events to announce. This can be an opportunity not only to promote your web site, but to educate patrons about new technology generally. In fact, promotion of your site almost implies that you will provide the training necessary to use it. Many patrons will be unfamiliar with Internet technology, or may have unrealistic expectations about it. It is important to present the site as another tool which patrons can use for their information needs, and for which the library will provide support. You might offer a series of workshops and demonstrations, perhaps as a part of the official web site kick-off. If you have a showcase or open house, take the time to display instructional sites, government information sites, and other resources that will interest patrons. Pique their interest by showing them these sites, letting them know that the technology is accessible, and demonstrating how it can be helpful to them personally. Offer them the opportunity to learn how to use it.

The series of follow-up workshops could include the things that you and your staff have been learning throughout the creation of the home page. These things should come easily to you now:

- An overview of the Internet, its history, its uses, and its potential.

- Specific instruction about the World Wide Web, and about hypertext and how it is used. Familiarize patrons with the terms that they see in news programs, magazines, and newspapers.

- How to use the technology involved. Demonstrate browsers, and talk about their availability. Tell them a little about connectivity.

- How to use the technology to specifically access your particular site (both from within your library building and remotely). Describe the information that your site contains. Provide instructional materials that they can take with them that will be applicable not only to your library's particular set up, but that will serve as reference material for them in the future.

Academic libraries can use sessions such as these to reach the departments on their campuses by structuring them around subject resources (Figure 6.3). For example, the Harlan Hatcher Graduate Library at the University of Michigan has initiated a series of two-hour classes designed to teach academic users how to find resources in their individual fields. Librarians experienced in Internet and World Wide Web use teach the first hour of each session, covering the basic techniques needed to navigate the Web. The second hour is led by the subject selector in that area, and focuses on WWW resources pertinent to the field.

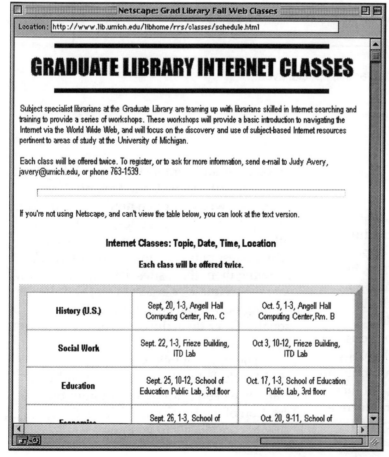

FIGURE 6.3
Academic library Internet classes that cover both web use and resources for pertinent subject areas

The WWW pages created to accompany these classes will be a part of the overall home page, thereby serving to publicize the classes and inform University users.

The Flint Model

More and more public libraries realize that a web site can be a valuable tool that needs to be publicized. They create web sites for their patrons that become focal points for accessing community information and they provide training to their users.

For example, the Flint Public Library (in collaboration with the University of Michigan's School of Information and Library Studies, the Mideastern Michigan Library Cooperative, and the U-M Flint Community Stabilization and Revitalization Project) has created the Flint Community Networking Initiative Training Center (Figure 6.4). They are providing "home-town

information available through their own community network linked to the Internet." (**http://www.sils.umich.edu/Publications/ CRISTALED/Flintcommnetwork.html**). The center's infrastructure incorporates the "first joint Merit/Ameritech ISDN installation, 18 linked Power Macintoshes, and supporting equipment and software; the vision for this space and equipment is that it will become a friendly meeting place which provides public access to the Internet, facilities for training a wide range of users, and a studio for the creation of community information resources." (**http://www.sils.umich.edu/ Publications/CRISTALED/ Pilotprojectsintro.html**).

Flint city government information appears on the web site, as well as information from county, state, and federal sources.

Area newspapers, radio stations, and television publicized the date of the formal dedication of the site. Interest in it was evidenced by the number of people who

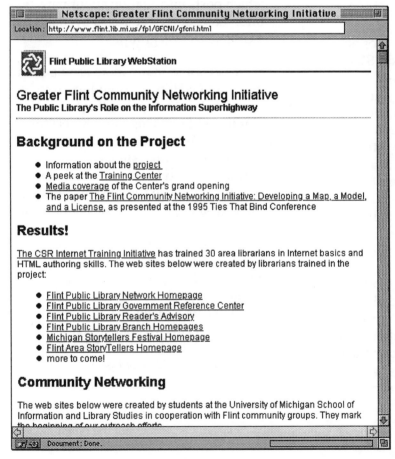

FIGURE 6.4
A web site that also serves as a center for community information

came to the grand opening ceremony. More than a hundred persons attended. This serves as one example of the interest in these types of resources, and the way public libraries can play a role in bringing them to their communities.

On the World Wide Web

In addition to reaching those in the immediate vicinity, you want to reach those who may be interested in using your resources remotely over the Internet. Publicizing a library web site throughout the Internet community can be pursued in several different ways. You will want to announce the debut of your site to the general WWW user population, and make it accessible in the catalogs of Internet subject directories and search engines. Doing this increases the chances of people finding your site when it has information they need.

Here are some places that you can start with:

- The "What's New with NCSA Mosaic" page (**http://www.ncsa.uiuc.edu/SDG/ Software/Mosaic/Docs/whats- new.html**) is one place where you can announce your web site when you feel it's ready for use. You can submit your entry through an online form (**http:// www.ncsa.uiuc.edu/SDG/Software/ Mosaic/Docs/whats-new-form.html**). "What's New with NCSA Mosaic" prefers to accept only content-rich web sites, and it usually takes ten to fourteen days to put up your information.

- Yahoo (**http//www.yahoo.com/**) offers a list of the new resources included in its database, usually for the most recent week. Its form (**http://www.yahoo.com/ bin/add/**) allows you to add your site to the appropriate category, along with your title, URL, and a short description.

- The Netscape "What's New Submission Form" (**http://home.netscape.com/ escapes/submit_new.html**) is a similarly styled form used to submit a description of your site for inclusion in Netscape's pages of new resources.

- Lycos (**http://fuzine.mt.cs.cmu.edu/ mlm/lycos-register.html**) accepts nominations of URLs for exploration. It accepts these registrations as recommendations for sites to consider.

- WebCrawler (**http://www.submit- it.com/**) accepts submissions of multiple URLs at one time and will take up to a week for the system to include your URL.

- You also might find listservs and news groups such as Gleason Sackman's net-happenings (see **http:// www.mid.net/net/** for subscription information) useful. This is a listserv which posts information about new Internet resources. It is also available as a USENET news group.

These sites and many more can be found at EPages' "FAQ: How to Announce Your New Web Site" (**http://ep.com/faq/ webannounce.html**). This site is an HTML version of the FAQ posted regularly to the news group **comp.infosystems. www.announce**, and is valuable in that it provides direct links to the sites that are high in popularity and use. It includes pointers to:

- What's New Web Pages
- Web Directory Pages
- Web Search Engines
- Newsgroups
- .Newsletters & Mailing Lists
- Books that have Web sites listed
- Magazines that have Web sites listed
- Miscellaneous, Lists of Lists

Measuring Your Success

Hopefully, as you publicize your site and provide training in its use, you will find that your audience is expanding and changing. You will need to evaluate and reevaluate your site to discover areas that you can change and improve to meet the needs of this changing audience. Evaluation, of course, can be seen as part of the maintenance process, and, like maintenance, should be planned for in the early stages of the project.

What are the signs of a successful web site? Evaluation will help you answer this question as you discover areas that are used profitably and other areas that may need to be changed or expanded. As with any new library service, a web site should be evaluated for its value to your library and its value to your patrons.

Value to Your Library

There are several ways to measure the value of your web site to your library. One of the most obvious areas is economics—how much the web site costs in terms of money. This includes the cost of equipment, staff time spent on the project, and miscellaneous expenses such as promotional materials. Keep track of these expenses as the project progresses. Decide if the outlay is excessive or moderate for the service provided.

A second area in which to evaluate the web site is in terms of staff development. If staff development was one of your goals, make to sure to follow up with the staff members who worked on the project, and those who make use of the site, and investigate how the site has affected them. If staff attended Internet workshops, ask them to describe how they have used the skills which they have acquired. If you have geared a section of the web site toward use by staff members, you might want to convene a focus group of staff to discuss how they use it and

what other information might be included. Very likely computing and Internet skills will have improved throughout the organization.

A third area to evaluate is the usefulness of the site in comparison to the other resources in the library. Examine the information included on the site to determine which areas have been ineffective in a WWW format, and which have been successful. For example, you may decide that creating a WWW list of new acquisitions is too time-consuming because it has to be updated so frequently, and therefore decide you will maintain only a paper version. On the other hand, some resources found online may be even more up to date and useful than print versions. This can be especially true of government documents, which change often and are usually more up to date in electronic form (Figure 6.5).

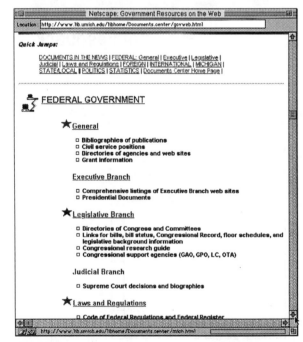

FIGURE 6.5
Government documents are usually more up to date in online form than in print versions.

Evaluating the Value to Your Patrons

Evaluating the value of the web site to your patrons may be more difficult to accomplish than evaluating its value to the staff, especially because your patrons may be accessing it from a remote location.

If you do provide in-library access to your web site, you may be able to survey patrons using an in-house print form placed by the workstation. More useful might be a feedback form added to your library web site which would be used to solicit suggestions for Internet resources and general comments on using the site. It can be as simple as a "mailto" tag or as complex as fill-out forms. You can insert a "mailto" tag on your page to facilitate feedback from users, but even better would be a feedback form soliciting specific evaluative information, asking for comments on such things as ease of use, usefulness of information, and overall design (Figure 6.6).

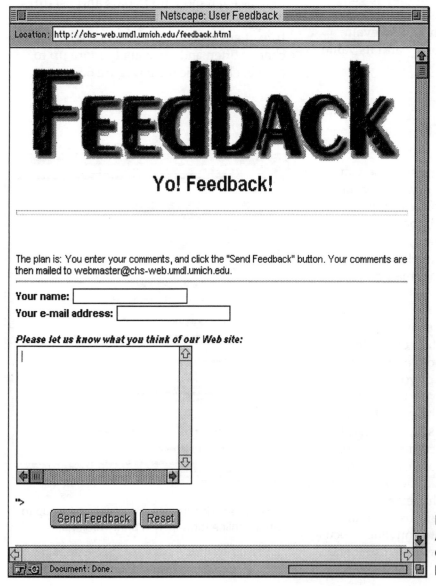

FIGURE 6.6
A feedback form solicits evaluative information from patrons about your web site.

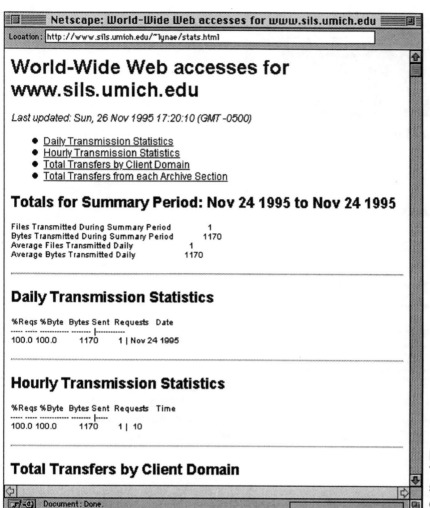

FIGURE 6.7
The use of system statistics software can also be helpful in evaluating your web site.

It might also be possible to form a focus group of users to evaluate your site. If your library board includes users from the community, they might be willing to participate in such a group. If you have student workers within your library, you could survey them. It should not be a hard to find local patrons who use your site and who would be willing to let you know what they think about it.

System statistics may also help you assess use of the web site (Figure 6.7). Some currently available system statistics packages come in the form of UNIX scripts that can be installed on your server by your system administrator. One of these is wwwstat (**http://www.ics.uci.edu/WebSoft/wwwstat/**),

UNIX public domain software written by Roy Fielding (**fielding@ics.uci.edu**) as part of the Arcadia project at the University of California, Irvine. This program uses the access log files on your server to output a summary of uses, already tagged with HTML and ready for display.

As you can see, some of the information, such as the "Daily Transmission Statistics," "Hourly Transmission Statistics," and "Total Transfers by Client Domain" reveals interesting use patterns regarding total number of uses, number of uses from a specific domain, and number of uses during a specific time period that could be taken into account when evaluating your web site.

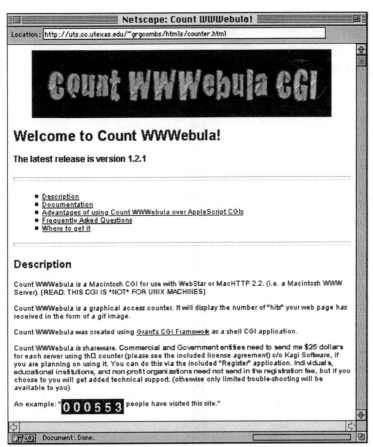

FIGURE 6.8
Count WWWebula, a system statistics application available for use as shareware

Other applications are being developed which would allow someone with less specialized knowledge to keep track of access statistics. For example, "Count WWWebula is a Macintosh CGI for use with WebStar or MacHTTP 2.2. (i.e., a Macintosh WWWServer)." (**http://uts.cc.utexas.edu/ ~grgcombs/htmls/counter.html**) This program is shareware that is free to individuals, educational institutions, and nonprofit organizations (currently $25 to others). It produces an odometer-like counter that tells you the total number of people who have accessed your site (Figure 6.8).

Your Presence on the Internet

One of the things mentioned at the beginning of this book was the value of establishing a web presence. How can you measure this? The e-mail you get, the mention of your resources on other sites, the prestige of having resources that others rely on, all of these things are signs that your site is being recognized and is becoming a resource that others look for.

Maintaining Your Site

To become a respected resource, a library web site, whether it is a simple home page or a more complex site, requires maintenance. As basic library information changes, information such as hours and phone numbers need to be updated. New resources that you will want to link to will be developed and sometimes resources that you have included will disappear. In addition, as network technology and standards change, the organization and layout of your site will need to be updated. A home page or web site becomes useless if the information it contains is not up to date, and visitors will not return if it is not refreshed periodically.

Because of all of these potential areas of change, maintaining a home page can become a complex process. All of the elements of your home page will need updating at varying times and to various degrees, so you will need to be prepared. As a first step, try to list the tasks you need to keep up with, and estimate how often these tasks will need to be done. These can include:

- updating local information

- checking hyperlinks

- adding new or deleting dead Internet resources

- reorganizing or changing design

Updating Local Information

Library hours, staff information, and contact information should be updated as often as needed, and you probably have a sense for the frequency of these changes. In an academic library, for instance, checking every semester would make sense. In a school library, the school calendar will reflect the times most likely to experience change. Public libraries also benefit from a periodic check. The more information you have added to this section, of course, the more details you should add to your list.

In addition to updating basic information as-needed, you will need to maintain your added features. If a web site includes local information such as event schedules, minutes of board meetings, or lists of new acquisitions, a regular schedule for updating this information should be implemented

as well. Depending on the type of information, updating may be needed once a week (new books list), once a month (calendar of events), or seasonally (community information).

Checking Hyperlinks

If you are linking to local files (those WWW documents which your library has created and which reside on your own server site), the location and URLs of these links will probably remain constant and will require minimal updating. If, however, you create a more complex web site and include links to resources maintained at other sites, you will need to check them regularly to ensure the validity of the path information, that the names of the resources haven't changed, or even that the resources still exist. A good rule of thumb would be to run through your links once a month to make sure they all work or to see if any of them have moved to new locations.

Recently, automated link-checkers have become available. The ones that we have looked at are UNIX programs that need to be installed by system administrators. These programs can make the task of checking links less time-consuming, but you should still make sure that they are run regularly.

Some link-checkers currently available are:

- WWW Link Checker (UNIX versions) — "When checker starts, it searches through your page and looks for links. As soon as it finds one, it will try to follow this link. If it cannot follow the link, that means the link probably invalid. Checker will display one line message for both valid and invalid links. Checker can handle most popular protocols HTTP, FTP, telnet, gopher ..." (**http://www.ugrad.cs.ubc.ca/spider/ q7f192/branch/checker.html**)

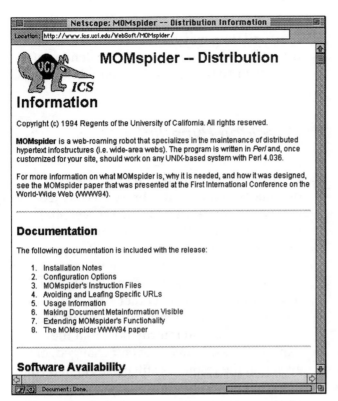

FIGURE 6.9
MOMspider, a link-checking program
available as shareware

- lvrfy: A HTML Link Verifier — "lvrfy is a script that verifies all the internal links in HTML pages on your server. Its operation is rather simple: it starts with one page, parses all the links (including inline images), and then recursively checks all the links." (**http://www.cs.dartmouth.edu/~crow/lvrfy.html**)

For complex structures that consist of multiple sites, MOMspider (Multi-Owner Maintenance spider) (Figure 6.9) "can periodically traverse a list of webs (by owner, site, or document tree), check each web for any changes which may require its owner's attention, and build a special index document that lists out the attributes and connections of the web in a form that can itself be traversed as a hypertext document." (**http://www.ics.uci.edu/WebSoft/MOMspider/WWW94/paper.html**).

Adding New/Deleting Old Internet Resources

Adding and removing resources will be a large part of the maintenance of most web sites. Internet resource collections need to be kept up to date. If you discover problems with the links that you have checked, you will need to either correct the problem or remove the links. New resource discovery in all subject areas should take place continually. If you maintain a subject resource list, resources that are no longer valuable will need to be removed.

Keeping up with new resources can be challenging, but there are many places where you can look for help (Figure 6.10). In addition to periodically searching the sites mentioned in Chapter 4, keep checking the announcement services mentioned at the beginning of this chapter.

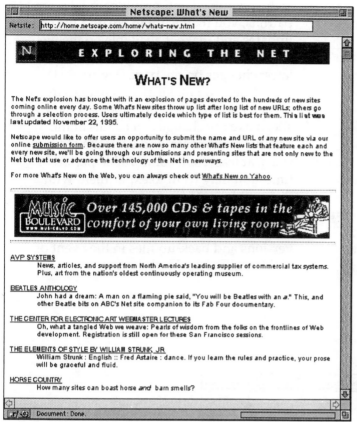

FIGURE 6.10

For site maintenance, an announcement service may be helpful when evaluating which new Internet resources to include.

Reorganizing and Changing Design

As Internet technology and styles change, reorganizing and changing the design of your web site will become a regular maintenance task. Perhaps the most important changes in this area will come in the imminent development of standards for the design and organization of WWW documents. Standards for HTML 3.0, the most potentially influential development, are forthcoming. Currently, most HTML authors employ tags from an older version of HTML. HTML, if applied strictly, can be conformable to the overall grammar, or standard, of SGML, the international Standard Generalized Markup Language. Most web documents are not constructed with this correct grammar in mind. The HTML 3.0 specification, as it is refined into a formal standard, will provide

some new features that will be displayable by all HTML 3.0-compliant browsers. Since this is expected to be a standard, the effects of using the new features will become commonplace, and more stable than using some of the browser-specific tags currently available.

Some of the proposed features that HTML 3.0 will support are customized lists, forms, a static banner area for standard toolbar/menu items (such as "back" and "next" buttons), and extended form capabilities. Again, to be strictly correct, these will need to be used according to the guidelines of the grammar.

Changes in browser technology will also drive the look of your pages. Currently, designing a document that looks good when viewed by the many different browsers available to WWW users is a challenge. New browsers will be developed, but whether they will become more or less standard remains to be seen. You can keep up with

71

new browsers and new versions of existing browsers by periodically checking in on the BrowserWatch page (**http://www.ski.mskcc.org/browserwatch**/), a site that collects announcements about changes in this area.

Tips for Maintenance

Keep a maintenance schedule. Plan ahead for maintenance, perhaps using a monthly calendar to target which areas of the web site you will update on which days. When adding a new section to your home page, note how often that resource will need updating.

To help yourself and provide updates for patrons, you may want to create a list of updates and make it available on the web site. And, once again, make sure to date the latest changes on the page (Figure 6.11).

When you make major changes in the organization, design, or content of the web site, make the changes on copies of the original documents, and keep the old versions, at least for a comfortable period of time. You may want to experiment with different layouts for documents, and want to go back to the originals, or use elements from previous versions. Also, keep old versions and back-up files in the event of accidentally deleted files.

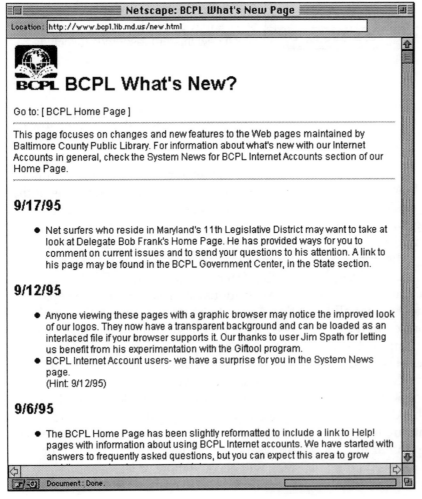

FIGURE 6.11
A maintenance schedule can also be put up as an announcement calendar.

Who Will Maintain the Site?

Perhaps the most important issue to address when planning for the maintenance of your site is who will be responsible for it. This is a question best answered before the web site construction has begun. Staff will want to know and be reassured that they will or will not be expected to take part in maintenance of the site, depending on their desired level of involvement. People involved in the development of the project would already be familiar with the technology and goals for the project; however, if those staff members cannot continue working on the project with the same level of participation, try to tap them as maintenance coordinators. Their expertise could then be passed on to another group or individual.

No matter who you choose to continue maintenance of the project, try to enlist the efforts of someone with long-term availability. Be careful about using students or other temporary employees. Their skills and expertise should be employed in the project, but turnover for these staff members could adversely affect long-term plans for maintenance.

We have had experience with two basic models for the maintenance of a web site, the first of which we call a centralized model and the second a decentralized model. Both of these approaches have their advantages and disadvantages, but each one is workable, and useful in the appropriate situation.

Centralized Approach to Web Site Maintenance

The centralized model to web maintenance is a situation in which one individual or one team will be primarily responsible for maintenance. This could work in a large academic library where a specific person or team will be hired full-time to maintain the site, or in a small public or school library where one person has been responsible for the creation of the web site and will continue to keep it

up. The centralized approach to web site maintenance provides more continuity throughout the life of the project, and more control over it in the hands of one person or group of people. This control can make it easier to keep design and organization consistent throughout the web site.

Centralized maintenance also means less investment in training time and physical resources. Only one or a few staff members will need the advanced training required to develop additional features. Less time will be needed for communication between those working on the page, and, on a practical level, fewer computer workstations will be needed for staff.

A disadvantage of having a single person or team responsible for style and content decisions is a possible narrowness of vision. It would be easy for one person, or even a small group of people, to overlook information outside their realm of expertise, or in which they are simply not interested. We recommend that if a centralized maintenance model is used, the web site maintainer should actively seek input and advice from other staff members and from patrons. Another concern regarding the centralized approach is that one person can become overwhelmed with maintenance work if this task is beyond this person's regular position. Maintaining a large or even medium-sized web site can be a full-time job.

Decentralized Approach to Web Site Maintenance

The decentralized approach involves spreading the responsibility of site maintenance among several units or individuals, each being responsible for only one section of the web site. Generally, this responsibility would be only one part of each individual's position. A decentralized approach may be implemented from the inception of a web site, but, more than likely, a basic site will first be constructed and then a decentralized maintenance model phased in later during the project.

When implementing a decentralized maintenance model, most of the responsibility for adding and updating information will be delegated to various units or staff members. Usually sections are handed over to those whose subject areas they cover, the obvious advantage to this being that they know their information best, and are best suited for the evaluation of new resources.

One possible disadvantage to this approach can be a loss of control over the look and content of the documents. Consistency is one of the goals you should strive for; giving over work to various units or people could contribute to a lack of recognizable elements. To avoid this potential problem, establish some sort of guiding policy for those involved in the maintenance of their specific pages. Similar to other library manuals, this policy can include expectations for updating links, a style sheet or template for pages, and helpful documents to assist the maintainers in their work. Such a manual can help keep individual pages consistent in style and content, but leave individuals enough room to be creative and express the uniqueness of their resources and services.

A decentralized maintenance model also makes staff turnover less of an issue. Chances are that more than one person in a unit will be familiar with the work done on the web site. Even if this is not the case, the delay while searching for someone to take over for a former staff member will only affect one section of the site. A decentralized approach also gives more people a chance to get involved and learn about web site construction and the Internet, and can provide a richer variety of information and ideas.

Appendix A

Online Resources

Library WWW Servers

Libweb: Library Information Servers via WWW
http://www.lib.washington.edu/~tdowling/libweb.html

 SJCPL's List of Public Libraries with Internet Services
http://sjcpl.lib.in.us/homepage/PublicLibraries/PublicLibraryServers.html

Digital Library Information

Digital Libraries - Resources and Projects
http://www.nlc-bnc.ca/ifla/services/diglib.htm

Background Materials about the Internet and WWW

Growth of the World Wide Web
http://www.netgen.com/info/growth.html

Falken's Cyberspace Tools
http://commline.com/falken/tools.shtml

Information Sources: the Internet and Computer-Mediated Communication
http://www.rpi.edu/Internet/Guides/decemj/internet-cmc.html

Internet Engineering Task Force Home Page
http://www.ietf.cnri.reston.va.us/home.html

Internet Society Home Page
http://info.isoc.org/

MIT World Wide Web Consortium
http://www.w3.org/

New User Directory
http://hcs.harvard.edu/~calvarez/newuser.html

Roadmap Workshop
http://ua1vm.ua.edu/~crispen/roadmap.html

Tools for Life on the Net
http://www.ee.pdx.edu/~rseymour/tools/

Understanding the Internet
http://www.screen.com/understand/start.nclk

WWW, HTML, Mosaic, etc.
http://www.bae.ncsu.edu:/bae/people/faculty/walker/hotlist/www.html

WWW InfoArea
http://www.netgen.com/infoarea/infoarea.html

World Wide Web FAQ
http://sunsite.unc.edu/boutell/faq/index.html

Internet Terminology

Free On-line Dictionary of Computing
http://wombat.doc.ic.ac.uk/

Glossary of Internet Terms
http://www.matisse.net/files/glossary.html

HTML Authoring

Authors & Webmasters: An Index of Resources at The Virtual Mirror
http://mirror.wwa.com/mirror/mirrind/htmlind.htm

A Beginner's Guide to HTML
http://www.ncsa.uiuc.edu/General/Internet/WWW/HTMLPrimer.html

HTML Reference Manual
http://www.sandia.gov/sci_compute/html_ref.html

Hypertext Markup Language (HTML): Working and Background
http://www.w3.org/hypertext/WWW/MarkUp/MarkUp.html

WWW Developer Resources
http://www.uwtc.washington.edu/Computing/WWW/Documentation.html

WWW Mailing Lists
http://www.w3.org/pub/WWW/Mail/Lists.html

Web Developer's Virtual Library
http://www.STARS.com/

Web Masters' Page (Bob Allison's Home Page)
http://gagme.wwa.com/~boba/masters1.html

Web4Lib Overview
http://www.lib.berkeley.edu/Web4Lib/

World Wide Web - tools for aspiring web weavers
http://www.nas.nasa.gov/NAS/WebWeavers/

OneWorld/SingNet WWW & HTML Developer's JumpStation
http://oneworld.wa.com/htmldev/devpage/dev-page1.html

Writing HTML, SGML, TEI
http://www.speakeasy.org/~dbrick/Hot/html.html

HTML Design

Art of HTML
http://www.thecoo.edu/~menon/html.html

Composing Good HTML
http://www.cs.cmu.edu/~tilt/cgh/

Elements of HTML Style
http://bookweb.cwis.uci.edu:8042/Staff/StyleGuide.html

HTML Design Notebook
http://www.w3.org/hypertext/WWW/People/Connolly/drafts/html-design.html

Principles of Good HTML Design
http://ugweb.cs.ualberta.ca/~gerald/guild/style.html

Roger's HTML Style Guide
http://www.york.ac.uk/~riws100/hobby/style.html

Yale WWW Style Manual
http://info.med.yale.edu/caim/StyleManual_Top.HTML

HTML Features

Extensions

Netscape Navigator Extensions to HTML

http://www.netscape.com/home/services_docs/html-extensions.html

Forms

CGI Form Handling in Perl
http://www.bio.cam.ac.uk/web/form.html

WebForms
http://www.q-d.com/wf.htm

Image Maps

Imagemap Help Page
http://www.hway.com/ihip/

MapMaker
http://tns-www.lcs.mit.edu/cgi-bin/mapmaker

Map THIS!
http://galadriel.ecaetc.ohio-state.edu/tc/mt/

NCSA Imagemap Tutorial
http://hoohoo.ncsa.uiuc.edu/docs/tutorials/imagemapping.html

WebMap for the Macintosh
http://www.city.net/cnx/software/webmap.html

HTML Link Checkers

MOMspider
http://www.ics.uci.edu/WebSoft/MOMspider/

lvrfy
http://www.cs.dartmouth.edu/~crow/lvrfy.html

HTML Standards

Document Type Definition for the HyperText Markup Language (HTML DTD)
http://www.w3.org/hypertext/WWW/MarkUp/html3/html3.txt

HTML 3.0 and Netscape 1.1N
http://ic.corpnet.com/~aking/webinfo/html3andns/

HyperText Markup Language Specification 3.0
http://www.hpl.hp.co.uk/people/dsr/html/Contents.html

HTML Validation

HALSoft HTML Validation Service
http://www.halsoft.com:80/html-val-svc/

WWWeblint
http://www.unipress.com/weblint/

Equipment & Software Resources

Browsers

BrowserWatch
http://www.ski.mskcc.org/browserwatch/

Connectivity

How To Select an Internet Service Provider
http://web.cnam.fr/Network/Internet-access/how_to_select.html

List of Internet Providers from Yahoo
http://www.yahoo.com/Business_and_Economy/Companies/
Internet_Access_Providers/

Server Software

An Information Provider's Guide to Web Servers
http://www.vuw.ac.nz/who/Nathan.Torkington/ideas/www-servers.html

MacHTTP/WebSTAR Home Page
http://www.starnine.com/machttp/machttpsoft.html

World Wide Web Server Software
http://www.w3.org/pub/WWW/Servers.html

Graphics Resources

Background Sampler
http://home.netscape.com/home/bg/

Free Art Site
http://www.mccannas.com/

Icon Browser
http://www.cli.di.unipi.it/iconbrowser/

Icons for Building Web Pages
http://www.jsc.nasa.gov/~mccoy/Icons/index.html

Sandra's Clip Art Server
http://www.cs.yale.edu/homes/sjl/clipart.html

Miscellaneous Software

General

SoftInfo, the ICP Software Information Center
http://www.icp.com/softinfo/

DOS/Windows

Downloadable Helper Applications for Windows
http://www.eden.com/music/winhelpers.html

MS-DOS Software via FTP
http://www.nova.edu/Inter-Links/software/dos.html

Oak Software Repository
http://www.acs.oakland.edu/oak.html

Macintosh

Search the University of Michigan Archives
http://www.tocnet.com/~baron/umich/

ULTIMATE Macintosh Sites
http://www.freepress.com/myee/ultimate_mac.html

Sites for Announcing New Web Sites

Add to Yahoo
http://www.yahoo.com/bin/top1?424,7

How to Announce Your New Web Site
http://ep.com/faq/webannounce.html

Lycos
http://fuzine.mt.cs.cmu.edu/mlm/lycos-register.html

What's New with NCSA Mosaic
http://www.ncsa.uiuc.edu/SDG/Software/Mosaic/Docs/whats-new-form.html

Sites for Locating New Resources

Best of the Web
http://wings.buffalo.edu/contest/

GNN Best of the Net Honorees
http://gnn.com/wic/botn/index.html

net-happenings
http://www.mid.net:80/net/

What's New on Yahoo
http://www.yahoo.com/bin/top1?23,8

Appendix B

Special Considerations for Academic Libraries

Although academic libraries are often best positioned in terms of technology, large academic institutions and their libraries are often more complex in terms of organizational structure. A decentralized organizational structure can make creating a central web site a challenge. Not only will it be harder to reach consensus about content and design, but it may be difficult to initiate such a project. In these situations, administrative support is especially important. Staff will need supervisors to approve the time they spend on the project, official sanction for the content may be needed, and managerial efforts will be especially important.

It will be a challenge to include resources for each library unit, as well as those supporting all academic departments of a university or college, which could be a very important political issue. In addition to serving the faculty, students, and staff well with your site, you do not want to alienate anyone whose interests may have been left out of your site. Striking a balance between available effort and web site coverage will be a critical issue.

Purpose/Audience

As with any library, academic libraries need to first consider their mission when beginning a web site project. A primary mission of an academic library is to support the curriculum of the academic institution. However, academic libraries range from those supporting small community colleges to large research institutions. The students will differ at these institutions, as will the curricula. You will need to match the content of your site to the needs of your patrons and staff. A community college library web site will most likely contain resources useful to students at a large university, but also might contain links to more vocational materials and community events. Always keep your audience in mind (Figure B.1).

Design and Construction of the Site

In a large institution, it is possible that a similar project may already be in the works.

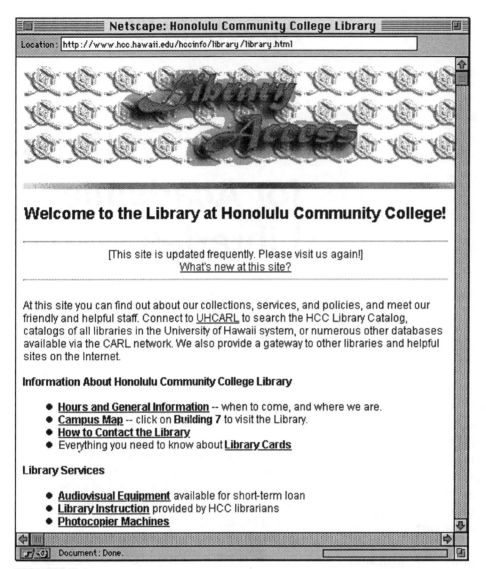

FIGURE B.1
A community college site contains resources that would be found in a
large university site, but content is carefully matched to patrons' needs.

Before starting a web site, become familiar with other projects going on in your library. Make sure that efforts are not being duplicated. You also may find it possible to join in with another interested staff member or group and share the workload of an already existing project. An academic library web site may also need to fit in with a larger campus site, so you will want to also look at projects which may be going on beyond the library. If you find other projects in progress on campus, you may be able to share resources and find a ready audience to give you feedback. Though the process may be very challenging, the variety of experience and interests present in an academic institution can be the base for a great web site.

Resources for Academic Librarians

Electronic Discussion Groups

- **NETTRAIN@UBVM.CC.BUFFALO.EDU**
  Network Trainers send the following
  e-mail message to
  LISTSERV@UBVM.CC.BUFFALO.EDU

  SUBSCRIBE NETTRAIN Your-first-name
  Your-last-name

  This list can also be read as a USENET
  news group at **bit.listserv.nettrain**

- **WEB4LIB@LIBRARY.BERKELEY.EDU**
  Library Web Site Design
  To subscribe to the list, send the following
  e-mail message to
  LISTSERV@LIBRARY.BERKELEY.EDU

SUBSCRIBE WEB4LIB Your-first-name
Your-last-name

For a complete collection of lists that
you might be interested in, check "Library-
Oriented Lists and Services" by Ann
Thornton and Steve Bonario (**http://
info.lib.uh.edu/liblists/home.htm**).

Web Sites

- **Libweb
  (http://www.lib.washington.edu/
  ~tdowling/libweb.html)**
  An excellent list of mostly academic
  library web sites around the world.

Appendix C

Special Considerations for School Library Media Centers

A school library media center is the perfect place from which to originate a school web site. A school library media center is the center for research, educational technology, and the information needs of students. School media specialists, perhaps more than any other librarians, have a very defined instructional role. Integrating Internet technology into the school library is a natural and important step. ICONnect (**http://ericir.syr.edu/ICONN/ihome.html**), a technology initiative coordinated by the American Association of School Librarians, has listed in their promotional materials the "Top Ten Reasons School Library Media Specialists Should Connect to the Internet":

1. Staff development opportunities

2. Empowerment for students

3. Availability of free instructional resources

4. Access to full-text resources

5. Creates credibility with other faculty members

6. Chance for experiential learning

7. Access to new software and technical information

8. New way to communicate with community members

9. Opportunity to participate in global dialogue

10. Terrific way to learn!

One of the easiest and most effective ways of connecting to the Internet is through the creation of a web site for your library. A school library web site will require special consideration in terms of purpose, audience, and content.

Purpose/Audience

The main consideration setting a school library media center web site apart from other library web sites is the purpose of the site. The mission of school libraries is to support the curriculum, to serve as a research

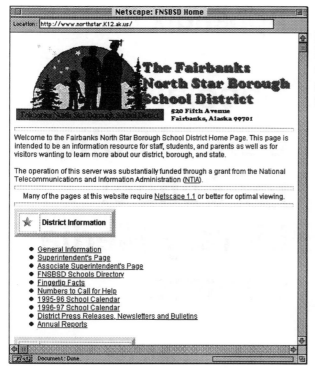

FIGURE C.1
In addition to the educational and recreational resources usually provided for students, this school web site also includes information relevant to parents.

FIGURE C.2
This school collaborates with the University of Michigan and the National Science Foundation for network access and equipment.

facility for faculty and students, and to serve the recreational information needs of students. This mission should be kept in mind when creating a media center web site. You will certainly want to include resources which support the curriculum, but you will also want to include some fun resources for students. Some school libraries' media centers have also included information of interest to parents (Figure C.1).

Equipment/Site Set-Up

As a school librarian, you may not have the good fortune of a direct Internet connection or high-end equipment. However, this does not mean that a web site is out of your reach. You may be able to work with a local college

or university, or purchase network service from a commercial organization. Community High School, in Ann Arbor, Michigan collaborates with the University of Michigan and the National Science Foundation to provide network access and equipment to their students (Figure C.2).

Design and Construction of the Site

A school library media center web site is most likely to be a part of an overall school web site. Creating a web site that is intended to fit in with a larger institutional site can have implications in terms of site design and construction. The most important part of creating such a site will be coordination of their pages. Since each of these pages will be a part of the larger school site, the designers may want to get together and decide on some standards for the pages. For example, to keep continuity throughout the site, the web designers might decide to make similar headers or toolbars for each page. On the other hand, the designers may decide similar headers and toolbars are not necessary to keep the look of the pages similar, but that the pages should each contain similar basic information, such as a contact person for the site or a date of last modification. No matter what the designers decide, this type of collaboration can be a very positive element of creating a good school web site.

Another area which makes a school library media center web site unique among library web sites is who may be creating the web site. It would be great to get faculty involved in the planning and selecting of content for the site. However, for a school library web site, we encourage you to get students involved in some aspect of the web project. In this way the construction of the site will serve as an educational experience, and might even be worked into the curriculum as a class project. Another positive effect of getting students involved will be sharing of the work involved. Also, students can take on different roles with regard to the site. One student who may not be interested in technological tasks may be good with graphics. Another student may prefer to work on document tagging. Many students with several different skills can get involved with a web project.

Several different approaches can be taken to involve students in web site development. In addition to integrating the web site project into a class, there are several other ways to get students involved. Students working in the library may be the best people to target. You may even decide to recruit some students with some technical expertise, and make the web site their primary task. The project might also be developed as an extracurricular activity or club (Figure C.3).

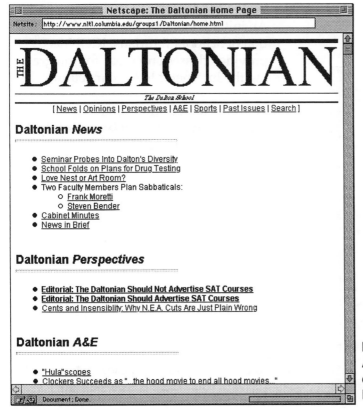

FIGURE C.3

A school publication with a web-savvy editor shows how student involvement helps make a web site work.

The project might also be developed as an extracurricular activity or club (Figure C.3).

In all of these approaches, it is important to keep in mind the educational aspect of web work. If students get involved, they will most likely need training and will definitely need support in their activities.

Policies

It will be very important to have a policy in place for a school library media center web site. Much current discussion centers around Internet resources and children. A policy for your site will give the students working on the page guidelines for their work, and will provide a usage policy for students who will access the site (Figure C.4).

Resources for School Librarians

Electronic Discussion Groups

- **LM_NET**
  To subscribe to LM_NET, send the

following message to **LISTSERV@LISTSERV.SYR.EDU:**

SUBSCRIBE LM_NET Your-first-name Your-last-name

For a complete collection of lists that you might be interested in, check "Library-Oriented Lists and Services" by Ann Thornton and Steve Bonario (**http://info.lib.uh.edu/liblists/home.htm**).

Web Design Information

- **Web66**
  (http://web66.coled.umn.edu/)
  A great list of all the school web sites in North America. Web66 also includes information on creating a web site and setting up a web server.

Integrating the Internet into the Curriculum

- **ICONnect**
  (http://ericir.syr.edu/ICONN/ihome.html)
  An initiative of the American Association of School Librarians. ICONnect provides classes and ideas for integrating the Internet into the curriculum.

- **WebEd Curriculum Links**
  (http://www.state.wi.us/agencies/dpi/www/WebEd.html)
  A large list of subject-oriented curriculum links.

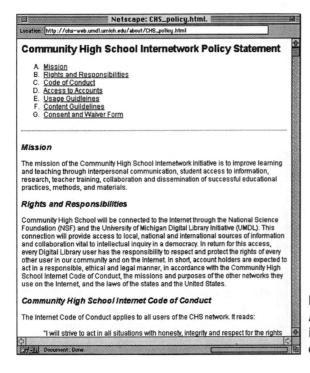

FIGURES C.4
An example of a school web site policy that includes a code of conduct and guidelines for content and usage

Appendix D

Special Considerations for Public Libraries

It is the aim of public libraries to become a local and integral resource for meeting the information needs of their communities, and it is logical for them to be focal points for this information. They often, however, need to balance the need for traditional collections and facilities with the demand for new information technology. Creating a web site can be a way to achieve this balance in that it can combine the information from traditional resources with the latest technology.

Audience/Purpose

The users of a public library, even more than those of school and academic libraries, represent a wide range of ages. These diverse segments of the population vary greatly in their needs, and will cover the spectrum of young children, teenagers, parents, professionals, and senior citizens. However, public libraries have an advantage in that they generally have a community profile or history available which outlines demographic trends, community statistics, and library usage patterns. Knowing this infor-

mation can be invaluable as work on a web page is begun.

Equipment/Site Setup

More and more public libraries are finding ways to connect to the Web and provide equipment for their patrons. Basically, there are two approaches libraries can take in providing Internet access for their staff and patrons. They can either obtain dial-up service or purchase a direct connection.

The West Bloomfield Township Public Library provides dial-up access. Note the elements involved as their setup is described in their fall 1995 newsletter:

The system now has:

- an additional 15 dial in lines, bringing our total to 21

- a division of the telephone lines into two groups - one group going directly to the Internet and the other to the Library's databases of information

- a dial-back feature which ensures that only members of our community have access to the network

- passwording of registered individuals to enhance security

- the ability to provide graphical user interface access to the World Wide Web portion of the Internet through a PPP connection and faster 28.8 modems which replaced the older 9600 baud units

Providing dial-up access for users will require an account with your local telephone service provider, an adequate number of dial-up lines, connectivity software such as PPP, and modems. You will also need a system administrator to provide maintenance, passwords, and other support functions.

For an example of a library with a direct line, read the St. Joseph County Public Library description of the process of becoming one of the first public libraries with an Internet connection:

> In October 1993, SJCPL became one of the first public libraries in Indiana to be connected to the Internet. We are linked by a direct connection purchased from CICNet (out of Ann Arbor) Michigan and a leased T-1 line that runs from the main library to the Internet node at the University of Notre Dame. We have been surfing the world of cyberspace for over a year! This connection allows us to offer the Internet to our entire staff as well as the public. Currently, we have 6 public terminals at the main library—4 Power Macs and 2 Macintosh IIvx's—plus one Power Mac at each of the 7 branches. The branches use a commercial software product called Apple Remote Access Client to dial into our network; soon they will all

be connected by dedicated 56k lines to the Main Library's T-1 line. We spent 7 months training the staff before making the Internet available to the public and will begin classes for the public in March of 1995.

(**http://sjcpl.lib.in.us/homepage/Reference/ INTERNET.html**)

This library purchased a direct connection from a commercial provider, and has computer stations in its facilities as well as provision for dial-up access.

Providing these services makes organized training sessions a must. Part of your overall plan should be to provide scheduling for all age groups with resources chosen especially for them.

Design and Construction of the Site

There should be no lack of ideas for content within a public library. You can present children's services, adult services, information about Friends of the library, community resources, Internet tips—the list is endless. What you do want to keep in mind at all times is your *local* audience. If you focus on local WWW users and their needs, design issues will be more easily addressed. The Boulder Public Library is a good example of a site that has addressed all age groups appropriately (**http://bcn.boulder.co.us/ library/bpl/home.html**) (Figure D.1).

As the web site of a public library is representative of the entire library, it may be best in public libraries for staff from each department to work on individual sections. They can tailor their sections to the audience they know best.

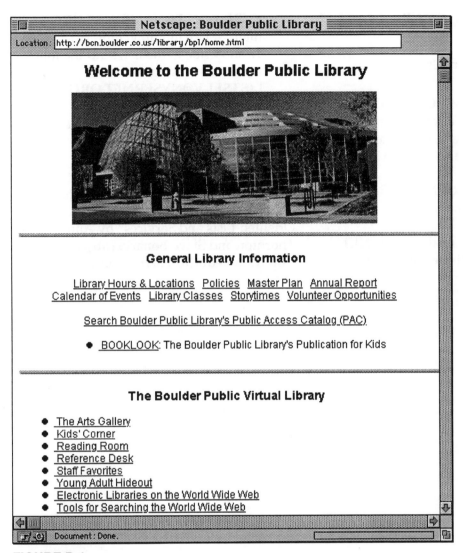

FIGURE D.1
A site that considers its local audience and addresses all age groups

Policies

Making Internet resources available to a wide range of users may call for some policies or disclaimers. The Westerville Public Library has this on its front page:

> The Internet service contains material of a controversial nature. In offering Internet access, the library staff cannot control access points which often change rapidly and unpredictably.

Patrons are hereby reminded that it is their responsibility for what access points are reached. Parents of minor children must assume responsibility for their children's use of the Internet in the Library.

(http://www.wpl.lib.oh.us/)

Other policies that you might want to set from the beginning may concern acceptable use of Internet accounts, or time limits for in-house use.

Resources for Public Librarians

Electronic Discussion Groups

- **NETTRAIN@UBVM.CC.BUFFALO.EDU**
  Internet/BITNET Network Trainers
  send the following e-mail message to
  LISTSERV@UBVM.CC.BUFFALO.EDU

  SUBSCRIBE NETTRAIN Your-first-name Your-last-name

  This list can also be read as a USENET news group at **bit.listserv.nettrain**.

- **PUBLIB-NET@NYSERNET.ORG**
  Internet Use in Public Libraries
  To subscribe to the list, send the following e-mail message to
  LISTSERV@NYSERNET.ORG

  SUBSCRIBE PUBLIB-NET Your-first-name Your-last-name

  For a complete collection of lists that you might be interested in, check "Library-Oriented Lists and Services" by Ann Thornton and Steve Bonario (**http://info.lib.uh.edu/liblists/home.htm**).

Appendix E

Home Page Templates

Home Page Template #1: Basic Approach

```
<HTML>
<HEAD>
<TITLE>Title of Page</TITLE>
</HEAD>

<BODY>

<H2>Home Page Template #1: Basic Approach</H2>
<HR>
<P>

<STRONG>Text introducing the library, who may use it, etc.</STRONG><P>

<H2>Basic Contact Information</H2>
<UL>
<LI>Address, phone, fax, e-mail
<LI>Hours
<LI>Contact people & information
</UL>

<H2>Resources</H2>
Text describing the scope of the library, collection size, formats available,
specialized materials, area strengths, collection plan, comparison to other
libraries, general horn-tooting, etc.

<H2>Services</H2>
Text about services
<UL>
<LI>(List of services)
</UL>

<HR>

<ADDRESS>Update information</ADDRESS>
</BODY>
</HTML>
```

Home Page Template #2: Value-Added Approach

```
<HTML>
<HEAD><TITLE>TITLE OF PAGE</TITLE></HEAD>

<BODY>
<H2>Home Page Template #2: Value-Added Approach</H2>
<HR>
<P>
<STRONG>Text introducing the library, who may use it, etc.
</STRONG>

<P>

<H2>Basic Contact Information</H2>
<UL>
<LI>Address, phone, fax, e-mail
<LI>Hours
<LI>Contact people & information
</UL>

<H2>Resources</H2>
Text describing the scope of the library, collection size, formats available,
specialized materials, area strengths, collection plan, comparison to other
libraries, general horn-tooting, etc.
<P>
<LI><strong>Local resources:</STRONG>
<P>
<UL>
<LI>(List of resources)
</UL>
<LI><strong>Internet resources:</STRONG>
<P>
<UL>
<LI>(List of resources)
</UL>
</UL>

<H2>Services</H2>
Text about services
<UL>(List of services)
<LI>
</UL>

<HR>
<ADDRESS>Update information</ADDRESS>

</BODY>
</HTML>
```

Home Page Template 3:
Extensive Service-Based Approach

```
<HTML>
<HEAD>
<TITLE>Title of Page</TITLE>
</HEAD>

<BODY>
<H1>Home Page Template 3: Extensive Service-Based Approach</H1>
<HR>

<H2>About the Library</H2>
Library hours, location (including directions and maps),
information about the Library's collections, and guide to floors.<P>

<H2>What's New!</H2>
<UL>
<LI> Electronic interlibrary loan forms
<LI> Library newsletter
<LI> Schedule of workshops being offered by the Library
</UL>

<H2>Reference Services</H2>
Hours, guide to reference collection, ask a reference question, and database
searching service.<P>

<H2>Circulation Services</H2>
Circulation and access policies, photocopy services, and the
Reserve Reading Room.<P>

<H2>Interlibrary Loan and Document Delivery Services</H2>
Forms for requesting materials not owned by the Library, and
instructions for faculty and researchers needing documents
delivered to their offices.<P>

<H2>Staff Directory</H2>
Staff directory, including telephone and e-mail numbers.<P>


<H2>Electronic Library Resources</H2>
Connect to library catalogs; guides to Internet resources.<P>

<HR>
<a href="mailto:library@example.address">Contact us</a>

<ADDRESS>Update information</ADDRESS>
</BODY>
</HTML>
```

Index

Page numbers in italics refer to illustrations.

About the Authors

Sherry Piontek and **Kristen Garlock** work for the University of Michigan's Digital Library Program. Their current project, JSTOR (Journal Storage Project), was established with the assistance of The Andrew W. Mellon Foundation and involves creating a digital archive of scholarly journals in various disciplines. Their position involves user support for JSTOR, Internet training, the creation of World Wide Web documents, and evaluation of materials on the Internet.

Sherry Piontek received her B.A. and her M.I.L.S. from the University of Michigan. Her previous WWW projects include the University Library Home Page and an experimental History of Art database.

Kristen Garlock received her undergraduate degree from Albion College and her M.I.L.S. from the University of Michigan. In addition to working on the University of Michigan Library Home Page, other projects have included the University of Michigan Information Gateway and Internet training for Michigan public librarians.